LAKE DISTRICT

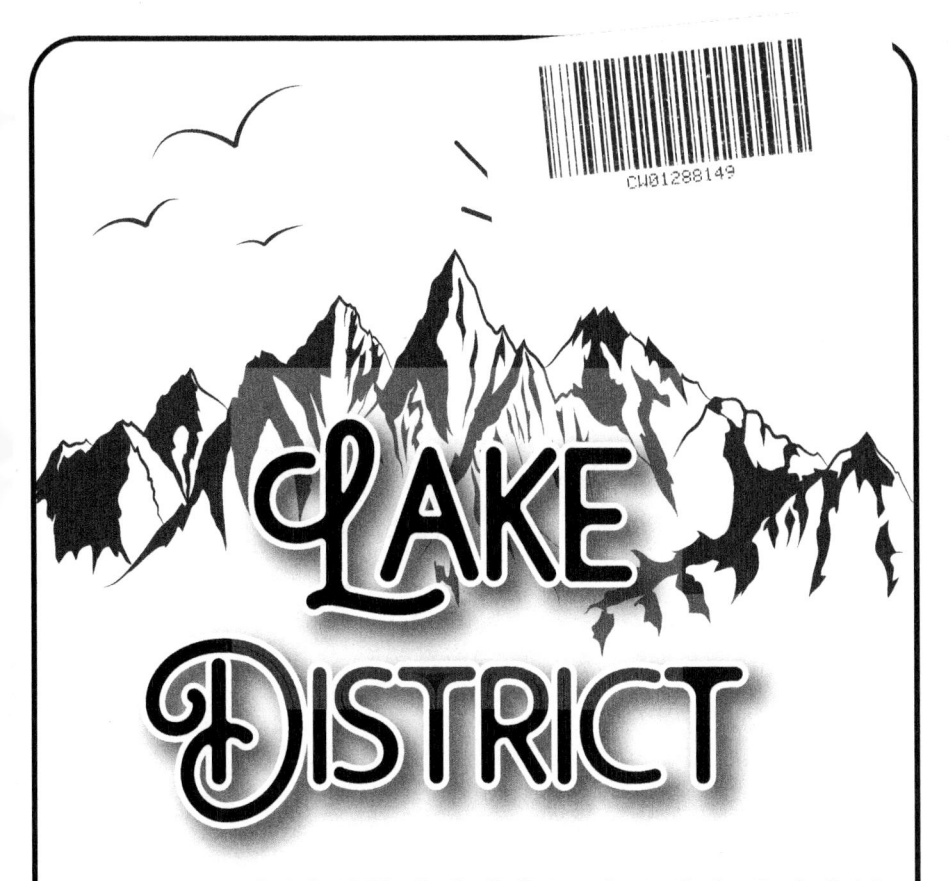

WAINWRIGHT BAGGING LOG BOOK
FOR FELL-WALKERS

Name: _____

Phone No: _____

Address: _____

_____

_____

Date: _____

© ADVENTURE PAL PUBLISHING

About this book,

This bagging log book has all the Wainwright peaks in the Lake District, listed in the ascending order of height(elevation). Unique layout of the book helps to record & log important information of each fell walk.

Wainwright Peak List - Ascending order of Heights
This section at the beginning of the book provides a quick way to search a particular peak and navigate through them easily. It also has a space to tick down the completed trails and provides a holistic view of all the peaks and height of them.

Wainwright Peak List - INDEX - Alphabetical Order
This section is ordered in the alphabetical order and is the quickest way to find a peak by its name.

Bagging Information Record & Log Section
This is the meat of the book and provides all the necessary parameters in a compact & effective layout to note down all the bagging information easily.

- Name of the Peak - Common name of the peak and alternative names where available
- Elevation/Height of the peak in "meters" and "feets"
- Region - In which part of the Lake District the peak is situated
- Parent Peak - Name of the parent peak that this peak belongs to
- OS Grid Reference to quickly locate the peak in the OS map

- Date of the peak bagging
- Space to record weather details
- Ascent Details - time starting, time at the peak & ascent duration
- Descent Details - time of descent start & finish and descent duration
- Total Duration & Distance of the trail

CASTLE CRAG		Region	North Western
290 m / 951 ft		OS Grid	NY249159
		Parent Peak	High Spy
Date		Weather Condition	
Ascent Start Time	Peak Time		Ascent Duration
Descent Start Time	Finish Time		Descent Duration
Notes	Total Duration		Total Distance
	Difficulty	1 2 3 4 5 6 7 8 9 10	
	Views	1 2 3 4 5 6 7 8 9 10	

- Ratings - 1 to 10 scale to rate the difficulty and views of the trail
- Note Area & extra note pages to record additional information, observations and special memories of the bagging.

Wainwright Peak List (Ascending Order of Height/Elevation)

Page	Peak Name	Height	Done	Page	Peak Name	Height	Done
7	Castle Crag	290 m	☐	34	Eagle Crag	525 m	☐
7	Holme Fell	317 m	☐	34	Gavel Fell	526 m	☐
8	Black Fell	323 m	☐	35	Great Cockup	526 m	☐
8	Loughrigg Fell	335 m	☐	35	Arthur's Pike	533 m	☐
9	Rannerdale Knotts	355 m	☐	36	Calf Crag	537 m	☐
9	High Rigg (Naddle Fell)	357 m	☐	36	Great Mell Fell	537 m	☐
10	Sale Fell	359 m	☐	37	Whin Rigg	537 m	☐
10	Troutbeck Tongue	364 m	☐	37	Blea Rigg	541 m	☐
11	Latrigg	368 m	☐	38	Lank Rigg	541 m	☐
11	Ling Fell	373 m	☐	38	Hard Knott	549 m	☐
12	Walla Crag	379 m	☐	39	Tarn Crag (Easedale)	549 m	☐
12	Hallin Fell	388 m	☐	39	Meal Fell	550 m	☐
13	Silver How	395 m	☐	40	Rosthwaite Fell	551 m	☐
13	Helm Crag	405 m	☐	40	Lord's Seat	552 m	☐
14	Fellbarrow (Mosser Fell)	416 m	☐	41	Steel Fell (Dead Pike)	553 m	☐
14	Grange Fell (Brund Fell)	416 m	☐	41	Knott Rigg	556 m	☐
15	Gibson Knott	420 m	☐	42	Brock Crags	561 m	☐
15	Buckbarrow	423 m	☐	42	Angletarn Pikes	567 m	☐
16	Low Fell	423 m	☐	43	Outerside	568 m	☐
16	Steel Knotts	432 m	☐	43	Sergeant's Crag	571 m	☐
17	Arnison Crag	433 m	☐	44	Blake Fell	573 m	☐
17	Glenridding Dodd	442 m	☐	44	Maiden Moor	575 m	☐
18	Binsey	447 m	☐	45	The Nab	576 m	☐
18	Great Crag	449 m	☐	45	Ard Crags	581 m	☐
19	Nab Scar	450 m	☐	46	Hartsop Above How	581 m	☐
19	Catbells	451 m	☐	46	Middle Fell	582 m	☐
20	Graystones	452 m	☐	47	Brae Fell	586 m	☐
20	Barrow	455 m	☐	47	Shipman Knotts	587 m	☐
21	Raven Crag	461 m	☐	48	Bleaberry Fell	590 m	☐
21	Barf	469 m	☐	48	Haystacks (Buttermere)	597 m	☐
22	Lingmoor Fell	470 m	☐	49	Seathwaite Fell	601 m	☐
22	Armboth Fell	475 m	☐	49	High Seat	608 m	☐
23	Burnbank Fell	475 m	☐	50	Illgill Head	609 m	☐
23	Gowbarrow Fell	481 m	☐	50	Heron Pike	612 m	☐
24	Longlands Fell	483 m	☐	51	Great Borne	616 m	☐
24	Sour Howes	483 m	☐	51	Hartsop Dodd	618 m	☐
25	Baystones (Wansfell)	487 m	☐	52	Birks	622 m	☐
25	Grike	488 m	☐	52	Yewbarrow	627 m	☐
26	Green Crag	489 m	☐	53	Mungrisdale Common	633 m	☐
26	Dodd	502 m	☐	53	Starling Dodd	633 m	☐
27	Stone Arthur	504 m	☐	54	Causey Pike	637 m	☐
27	Little Mell Fell	505 m	☐	54	Little Hart Crag	637 m	☐
28	Low Pike	508 m	☐	55	Grey Crag (Sleddale)	638 m	☐
28	Beda Fell (Beda Head)	509 m	☐	55	Base Brown	646 m	☐
29	Hen Comb	509 m	☐	56	Fleetwith Pike	649 m	☐
29	Broom Fell	511 m	☐	56	Great Sca Fell	651 m	☐
30	Mellbreak	512 m	☐	57	Rossett Pike	651 m	☐
30	High Tove	515 m	☐	57	High Spy	653 m	☐
31	Sallows	516 m	☐	58	Harter Fell (Eskdale)	654 m	☐
31	Whinlatter (Brown How)	517 m	☐	58	Middle Dodd	654 m	☐
32	High Hartsop Dodd	519 m	☐	59	Selside Pike	655 m	☐
32	Souther Fell	522 m	☐	59	High Pike (Scandale)	656 m	☐
33	Crag Fell	523 m	☐	60	Place Fell	657 m	☐
33	Bonscale Pike	524 m	☐	60	High Pike (Caldbeck)	658 m	☐

Wainwright Peak List (Ascending Order of Height/Elevation)

Page	Peak Name	Height	Done	Page	Peak Name	Height	Done
61	Whiteless Pike	660 m	☐	88	Wandope	772 m	☐
61	Carrock Fell	663 m	☐	88	Grey Friar	773 m	☐
62	Tarn Crag (Sleddale)	664 m	☐	89	Sail	773 m	☐
62	Wether Hill	671 m	☐	89	Red Screes	776 m	☐
63	Loadpot Hill	672 m	☐	90	Dow Crag	778 m	☐
63	Scar Crags	672 m	☐	90	Harter Fell (Mardale)	779 m	☐
64	Bakestall	673 m	☐	91	Kidsty Pike	780 m	☐
64	Sheffield Pike	675 m	☐	91	Glaramara	783 m	☐
65	Loft Crag	680 m	☐	92	Thornthwaite Crag	784 m	☐
65	Bannerdale Crags	683 m	☐	92	Allen Crags	785 m	☐
66	Great Calva	690 m	☐	93	Great Carrs	785 m	☐
66	Ullock Pike	690 m	☐	93	Watson's Dodd	789 m	☐
67	Seatallan	692 m	☐	94	Grisedale Pike	791 m	☐
67	Rest Dodd	696 m	☐	94	Dove Crag	792 m	☐
68	Caw Fell	697 m	☐	95	Rampsgill Head	792 m	☐
68	Grey Knotts	697 m	☐	95	Brim Fell	796 m	☐
69	Gray Crag	699 m	☐	96	Haycock	797 m	☐
69	Pavey Ark	700 m	☐	96	Green Gable	801 m	☐
70	Cold Pike	701 m	☐	97	High Raise (High Street)	802 m	☐
70	Bowscale Fell	702 m	☐	97	Kirk Fell	802 m	☐
71	Pike of Blisco	705 m	☐	98	Swirl How	802 m	☐
71	Yoke	706 m	☐	98	The Old Man of Coniston	802 m	☐
72	Whiteside (West Top)	707 m	☐	99	High Stile	806 m	☐
72	Pike of Stickle	709 m	☐	99	Lingmell	807 m	☐
73	Knott	710 m	☐	100	Steeple	819 m	☐
73	Branstree	713 m	☐	100	Hart Crag	822 m	☐
74	Brandreth	715 m	☐	101	Red Pike (Wasdale)	826 m	☐
74	Lonscale Fell	715 m	☐	101	High Street	828 m	☐
75	Birkhouse Moor	718 m	☐	102	Crag Hill (Eel Crag)	839 m	☐
75	Froswick	720 m	☐	102	Scoat Fell	841 m	☐
76	Thunacar Knott	723 m	☐	103	St Sunday Crag	841 m	☐
76	Clough Head	726 m	☐	103	Stybarrow Dodd	843 m	☐
77	Ullscarf	726 m	☐	104	Grasmoor	852 m	☐
77	Hindscarth	727 m	☐	104	Great Dodd	857 m	☐
78	Kentmere Pike	730 m	☐	105	Dollywaggon Pike	858 m	☐
78	Long Side	734 m	☐	105	Crinkle Crags (Long Top)	859 m	☐
79	Harrison Stickle	736 m	☐	106	White Side	863 m	☐
79	Sergeant Man	736 m	☐	106	Skiddaw Little Man	865 m	☐
80	Robinson	737 m	☐	107	Blencathra (Hallsfell Top)	868 m	☐
80	Seat Sandal	737 m	☐	107	Fairfield	873 m	☐
81	The Knott (High Street)	739 m	☐	108	Raise	883 m	☐
81	High Crag (Buttermere)	744 m	☐	108	Esk Pike	885 m	☐
82	Carl Side	746 m	☐	109	Catstye Cam	890 m	☐
82	Dale Head	753 m	☐	109	Nethermost Pike	891 m	☐
83	Red Pike (Buttermere)	755 m	☐	110	Pillar	892 m	☐
83	Hart Side	756 m	☐	110	Great Gable	899 m	☐
84	Ill Bell	757 m	☐	111	Bowfell	903 m	☐
84	Mardale Ill Bell	760 m	☐	111	Great End	910 m	☐
85	High Raise (Langdale)	762 m	☐	112	Skiddaw	931 m	☐
85	Slight Side	762 m	☐	112	Helvellyn	950 m	☐
86	Stony Cove Pike	763 m	☐	113	Scafell	964 m	☐
86	Wetherlam	763 m	☐	113	Scafell Pike	978 m	☐
87	Great Rigg	766 m	☐				
87	Hopegill Head	770 m	☐				

Wainwright Peak List - INDEX (Alphabetical Order)

Peak Name	Page	Peak Name	Page	Peak Name	Page
Allen Crags	92	Great Gable	110	Nethermost Pike	109
Angletarn Pikes	42	Great Mell Fell	36	Outerside	43
Ard Crags	45	Great Rigg	87	Pavey Ark	69
Armboth Fell	22	Great Sca Fell	56	Pike of Blisco	71
Arnison Crag	17	Green Crag	26	Pike of Stickle	72
Arthur's Pike	35	Green Gable	96	Pillar	110
Bakestall	64	Grey Crag (Sleddale)	55	Place Fell	60
Bannerdale Crags	65	Grey Friar	88	Raise	108
Barf	21	Grey Knotts	68	Rampsgill Head	95
Barrow	20	Grike	25	Rannerdale Knotts	9
Base Brown	55	Grisedale Pike	94	Raven Crag	21
Baystones (Wansfell)	25	Hallin Fell	12	Red Pike (Buttermere)	83
Beda Fell (Beda Head)	28	Hard Knott	38	Red Pike (Wasdale)	101
Binsey	18	Harrison Stickle	79	Red Screes	89
Birkhouse Moor	75	Hart Crag	100	Rest Dodd	67
Birks	52	Hart Side	83	Robinson	80
Black Fell	8	Harter Fell (Eskdale)	58	Rossett Pike	57
Blake Fell	44	Harter Fell (Mardale)	90	Rosthwaite Fell	40
Blea Rigg	37	Hartsop Above How	46	Sail	89
Bleaberry Fell	48	Hartsop Dodd	51	Sale Fell	10
Blencathra (Hallsfell Top)	107	Haycock	96	Sallows	31
Bonscale Pike	33	Haystacks (Buttermere)	48	Scafell	113
Bowfell	111	Helm Crag	13	Scafell Pike	113
Bowscale Fell	70	Helvellyn	112	Scar Crags	63
Brae Fell	47	Hen Comb	29	Scoat Fell	102
Brandreth	74	Heron Pike	50	Seat Sandal	80
Branstree	73	High Crag (Buttermere)	81	Seatallan	67
Brim Fell	95	High Hartsop Dodd	32	Seathwaite Fell	49
Brock Crags	42	High Pike (Caldbeck)	60	Selside Pike	59
Broom Fell	29	High Pike (Scandale)	59	Sergeant Man	79
Buckbarrow	15	High Raise (High Street)	97	Sergeant's Crag	43
Burnbank Fell	23	High Raise (Langdale)	85	Sheffield Pike	64
Calf Crag	36	High Rigg (Naddle Fell)	9	Shipman Knotts	47
Carl Side	82	High Seat	49	Silver How	13
Carrock Fell	61	High Spy	57	Skiddaw	112
Castle Crag	7	High Stile	99	Skiddaw Little Man	106
Catbells	19	High Street	101	Slight Side	85
Catstye Cam	109	High Tove	30	Sour Howes	24
Causey Pike	54	Hindscarth	77	Souther Fell	32
Caw Fell	68	Holme Fell	7	St Sunday Crag	103
Clough Head	76	Hopegill Head	87	Starling Dodd	53
Cold Pike	70	Ill Bell	84	Steel Fell (Dead Pike)	41
Crag Fell	33	Illgill Head	50	Steel Knotts	16
Crag Hill (Eel Crag)	102	Kentmere Pike	78	Steeple	100
Crinkle Crags (Long Top)	105	Kidsty Pike	91	Stone Arthur	27
Dale Head	82	Kirk Fell	97	Stony Cove Pike	86
Dodd	26	Knott	73	Stybarrow Dodd	103
Dollywaggon Pike	105	Knott Rigg	41	Swirl How	98
Dove Crag	94	Lank Rigg	38	Tarn Crag (Easedale)	39
Dow Crag	90	Latrigg	11	Tarn Crag (Sleddale)	62
Eagle Crag	34	Ling Fell	11	The Knott (High Street)	81
Esk Pike	108	Lingmell	99	The Nab	45
Fairfield	107	Lingmoor Fell	22	The Old Man of Coniston	98
Fellbarrow (Mosser Fell)	14	Little Hart Crag	54	Thornthwaite Crag	92
Fleetwith Pike	56	Little Mell Fell	27	Thunacar Knott	76
Froswick	75	Loadpot Hill	63	Troutbeck Tongue	10
Gavel Fell	34	Loft Crag	65	Ullock Pike	66
Gibson Knott	15	Long Side	78	Ullscarf	77
Glaramara	91	Longlands Fell	24	Walla Crag	12
Glenridding Dodd	17	Lonscale Fell	74	Wandope	88
Gowbarrow Fell	23	Lord's Seat	40	Watson's Dodd	93
Grange Fell (Brund Fell)	14	Loughrigg Fell	8	Wether Hill	62
Grasmoor	104	Low Fell	16	Wetherlam	86
Gray Crag	69	Low Pike	28	Whin Rigg	37
Graystones	20	Maiden Moor	44	Whinlatter (Brown How)	31
Great Borne	51	Mardale Ill Bell	84	White Side	106
Great Calva	66	Meal Fell	39	Whiteless Pike	61
Great Carrs	93	Mellbreak	30	Whiteside (West Top)	72
Great Cockup	35	Middle Dodd	58	Yewbarrow	52
Great Crag	18	Middle Fell	46	Yoke	71
Great Dodd	104	Mungrisdale Common	53		
Great End	111	Nab Scar	19		

Castle Crag

290 m / 951 ft

Region	North Western
OS Grid	NY249159
Parent Peak	High Spy

Date	Weather Condition

Ascent Start Time	Peak Time	Ascent Duration

Descent Start Time	Finish Time	Descent Duration

Notes

Total Duration	Total Distance

Difficulty [1] [2] [3] [4] [5] [6] [7] [8] [9] [10]
Views [1] [2] [3] [4] [5] [6] [7] [8] [9] [10]

Holme Fell

317 m / 1040 ft

Region	Southern
OS Grid	NY315006
Parent Peak	Old Man of Coniston

Date	Weather Condition

Ascent Start Time	Peak Time	Ascent Duration

Descent Start Time	Finish Time	Descent Duration

Notes

Total Duration	Total Distance

Difficulty [1] [2] [3] [4] [5] [6] [7] [8] [9] [10]
Views [1] [2] [3] [4] [5] [6] [7] [8] [9] [10]

Black Fell

323 m / 1060 ft

Region	Southern
OS Grid	NY340015
Parent Peak	Top o'Selside

Date	Weather Condition

Ascent Start Time	Peak Time	Ascent Duration

Descent Start Time	Finish Time	Descent Duration

Notes	Total Duration	Total Distance

Difficulty: (1) (2) (3) (4) (5) (6) (7) (8) (9) (10)
Views: (1) (2) (3) (4) (5) (6) (7) (8) (9) (10)

Loughrigg Fell

335 m / 1099 ft

Region	Central
OS Grid	NY346051
Parent Peak	High Raise

Date	Weather Condition

Ascent Start Time	Peak Time	Ascent Duration

Descent Start Time	Finish Time	Descent Duration

Notes	Total Duration	Total Distance

Difficulty: (1) (2) (3) (4) (5) (6) (7) (8) (9) (10)
Views: (1) (2) (3) (4) (5) (6) (7) (8) (9) (10)

Rannerdale Knotts

355 m / 1165 ft

Region	North Western
OS Grid	NY167182
Parent Peak	Crag Hill

Date	Weather Condition

Ascent Start Time	Peak Time	Ascent Duration

Descent Start Time	Finish Time	Descent Duration

Notes	Total Duration	Total Distance

Difficulty: (1) (2) (3) (4) (5) (6) (7) (8) (9) (10)
Views: (1) (2) (3) (4) (5) (6) (7) (8) (9) (10)

High Rigg (Naddle Fell)

357 m / 1171 ft

Region	Central
OS Grid	NY308219
Parent Peak	High Raise

Date	Weather Condition

Ascent Start Time	Peak Time	Ascent Duration

Descent Start Time	Finish Time	Descent Duration

Notes	Total Duration	Total Distance

Difficulty: (1) (2) (3) (4) (5) (6) (7) (8) (9) (10)
Views: (1) (2) (3) (4) (5) (6) (7) (8) (9) (10)

SALE FELL
359 m / 1178 ft

Region	North Western
OS Grid	NY194296
Parent Peak	Lord's Seat

Date	Weather Condition

Ascent Start Time	Peak Time	Ascent Duration

Descent Start Time	Finish Time	Descent Duration

Notes

Total Duration	Total Distance

Difficulty 1 2 3 4 5 6 7 8 9 10
Views 1 2 3 4 5 6 7 8 9 10

TROUTBECK TONGUE
364 m / 1194 ft

Region	Far Eastern
OS Grid	NY422064
Parent Peak	Froswick

Date	Weather Condition

Ascent Start Time	Peak Time	Ascent Duration

Descent Start Time	Finish Time	Descent Duration

Notes

Total Duration	Total Distance

Difficulty 1 2 3 4 5 6 7 8 9 10
Views 1 2 3 4 5 6 7 8 9 10

LATRIGG
368 m / 1207 ft

Region	Northern
OS Grid	NY279247
Parent Peak	Skiddaw

Date	Weather Condition

Ascent Start Time	Peak Time	Ascent Duration

Descent Start Time	Finish Time	Descent Duration

Notes

Total Duration	Total Distance

Difficulty [1] [2] [3] [4] [5] [6] [7] [8] [9] [10]
Views [1] [2] [3] [4] [5] [6] [7] [8] [9] [10]

LING FELL
373 m / 1224 ft

Region	North Western
OS Grid	NY179285
Parent Peak	Lord's Seat

Date	Weather Condition

Ascent Start Time	Peak Time	Ascent Duration

Descent Start Time	Finish Time	Descent Duration

Notes

Total Duration	Total Distance

Difficulty [1] [2] [3] [4] [5] [6] [7] [8] [9] [10]
Views [1] [2] [3] [4] [5] [6] [7] [8] [9] [10]

WALLA CRAG
379 m / 1243 ft

Region	Central
OS Grid	NY276212
Parent Peak	Bleaberry Fell

Date	Weather Condition

Ascent Start Time	Peak Time	Ascent Duration

Descent Start Time	Finish Time	Descent Duration

Notes

Total Duration	Total Distance

Difficulty [1] [2] [3] [4] [5] [6] [7] [8] [9] [10]
Views [1] [2] [3] [4] [5] [6] [7] [8] [9] [10]

HALLIN FELL
388 m / 1273 ft

Region	Far Eastern
OS Grid	NY433198
Parent Peak	High Street

Date	Weather Condition

Ascent Start Time	Peak Time	Ascent Duration

Descent Start Time	Finish Time	Descent Duration

Notes

Total Duration	Total Distance

Difficulty [1] [2] [3] [4] [5] [6] [7] [8] [9] [10]
Views [1] [2] [3] [4] [5] [6] [7] [8] [9] [10]

Silver How

395 m / 1296 ft

Region	Central
OS Grid	NY324066
Parent Peak	Harrison Stickle

Date	Weather Condition

Ascent Start Time	Peak Time	Ascent Duration

Descent Start Time	Finish Time	Descent Duration

Notes

Total Duration	Total Distance

Difficulty: [1] [2] [3] [4] [5] [6] [7] [8] [9] [10]
Views: [1] [2] [3] [4] [5] [6] [7] [8] [9] [10]

Helm Crag

405 m / 1329 ft

Region	Central
OS Grid	NY326093
Parent Peak	High Raise

Date	Weather Condition

Ascent Start Time	Peak Time	Ascent Duration

Descent Start Time	Finish Time	Descent Duration

Notes

Total Duration	Total Distance

Difficulty: [1] [2] [3] [4] [5] [6] [7] [8] [9] [10]
Views: [1] [2] [3] [4] [5] [6] [7] [8] [9] [10]

Fellbarrow (Mosser Fell)

416 m / 1365 ft

Region	Western
OS Grid	NY132242
Parent Peak	Low Fell

Date	Weather Condition

Ascent Start Time	Peak Time	Ascent Duration

Descent Start Time	Finish Time	Descent Duration

Notes

Total Duration	Total Distance

Difficulty: 1 2 3 4 5 6 7 8 9 10
Views: 1 2 3 4 5 6 7 8 9 10

Grange Fell (Brund Fell)

416 m / 1365 ft

Region	Central
OS Grid	NY264162
Parent Peak	Great Crag

Date	Weather Condition

Ascent Start Time	Peak Time	Ascent Duration

Descent Start Time	Finish Time	Descent Duration

Notes

Total Duration	Total Distance

Difficulty: 1 2 3 4 5 6 7 8 9 10
Views: 1 2 3 4 5 6 7 8 9 10

GIBSON KNOTT
420 m / 1378 ft

Region	Central
OS Grid	NY316100
Parent Peak	Calf Crag

Date	Weather Condition

Ascent Start Time	Peak Time	Ascent Duration

Descent Start Time	Finish Time	Descent Duration

Notes	Total Duration	Total Distance

Difficulty: [1] [2] [3] [4] [5] [6] [7] [8] [9] [10]
Views: [1] [2] [3] [4] [5] [6] [7] [8] [9] [10]

BUCKBARROW
423 m / 1388 ft

Region	Western
OS Grid	NY135061
Parent Peak	Seatallan

Date	Weather Condition

Ascent Start Time	Peak Time	Ascent Duration

Descent Start Time	Finish Time	Descent Duration

Notes	Total Duration	Total Distance

Difficulty: [1] [2] [3] [4] [5] [6] [7] [8] [9] [10]
Views: [1] [2] [3] [4] [5] [6] [7] [8] [9] [10]

LOW FELL
423 m / 1388 ft

Region	Western
OS Grid	NY137226
Parent Peak	High Stile

Date	Weather Condition

Ascent Start Time	Peak Time	Ascent Duration

Descent Start Time	Finish Time	Descent Duration

Notes

Total Duration	Total Distance

Difficulty [1] [2] [3] [4] [5] [6] [7] [8] [9] [10]
Views [1] [2] [3] [4] [5] [6] [7] [8] [9] [10]

STEEL KNOTTS
432 m / 1417 ft

Region	Far Eastern
OS Grid	NY440181
Parent Peak	High Raise

Date	Weather Condition

Ascent Start Time	Peak Time	Ascent Duration

Descent Start Time	Finish Time	Descent Duration

Notes

Total Duration	Total Distance

Difficulty [1] [2] [3] [4] [5] [6] [7] [8] [9] [10]
Views [1] [2] [3] [4] [5] [6] [7] [8] [9] [10]

ARNISON CRAG

433 m / 1421 ft

Region	Eastern
OS Grid	NY393149
Parent Peak	Birks

Date	Weather Condition

Ascent Start Time	Peak Time	Ascent Duration

Descent Start Time	Finish Time	Descent Duration

Notes	Total Duration	Total Distance

Difficulty: ① ② ③ ④ ⑤ ⑥ ⑦ ⑧ ⑨ ⑩
Views: ① ② ③ ④ ⑤ ⑥ ⑦ ⑧ ⑨ ⑩

GLENRIDDING DODD

442 m / 1450 ft

Region	Eastern
OS Grid	NY380175
Parent Peak	Sheffield Pike

Date	Weather Condition

Ascent Start Time	Peak Time	Ascent Duration

Descent Start Time	Finish Time	Descent Duration

Notes	Total Duration	Total Distance

Difficulty: ① ② ③ ④ ⑤ ⑥ ⑦ ⑧ ⑨ ⑩
Views: ① ② ③ ④ ⑤ ⑥ ⑦ ⑧ ⑨ ⑩

BINSEY
447 m / 1467 ft

Region	Northern
OS Grid	NY225355
Parent Peak	Knott

Date	Weather Condition

Ascent Start Time	Peak Time	Ascent Duration

Descent Start Time	Finish Time	Descent Duration

Notes

Total Duration	Total Distance

Difficulty	[1] [2] [3] [4] [5] [6] [7] [8] [9] [10]
Views	[1] [2] [3] [4] [5] [6] [7] [8] [9] [10]

GREAT CRAG
449 m / 1473 ft

Region	Central
OS Grid	NY270146
Parent Peak	Ullscarf

Date	Weather Condition

Ascent Start Time	Peak Time	Ascent Duration

Descent Start Time	Finish Time	Descent Duration

Notes

Total Duration	Total Distance

Difficulty	[1] [2] [3] [4] [5] [6] [7] [8] [9] [10]
Views	[1] [2] [3] [4] [5] [6] [7] [8] [9] [10]

NAB SCAR
450 m / 1476 ft

Region	Eastern
OS Grid	NY355072
Parent Peak	Heron Pike

Date	Weather Condition

Ascent Start Time	Peak Time	Ascent Duration

Descent Start Time	Finish Time	Descent Duration

Notes	Total Duration	Total Distance
	Difficulty	(1) (2) (3) (4) (5) (6) (7) (8) (9) (10)
	Views	(1) (2) (3) (4) (5) (6) (7) (8) (9) (10)

CATBELLS
451 m / 1480 ft

Region	North Western
OS Grid	NY244198
Parent Peak	Dale Head

Date	Weather Condition

Ascent Start Time	Peak Time	Ascent Duration

Descent Start Time	Finish Time	Descent Duration

Notes	Total Duration	Total Distance
	Difficulty	(1) (2) (3) (4) (5) (6) (7) (8) (9) (10)
	Views	(1) (2) (3) (4) (5) (6) (7) (8) (9) (10)

GRAYSTONES
452 m / 1483 ft

Region	North Western
OS Grid	NY176266
Parent Peak	

Date	Weather Condition

Ascent Start Time	Peak Time	Ascent Duration

Descent Start Time	Finish Time	Descent Duration

Notes

Total Duration	Total Distance

Difficulty: [1] [2] [3] [4] [5] [6] [7] [8] [9] [10]
Views: [1] [2] [3] [4] [5] [6] [7] [8] [9] [10]

BARROW
455 m / 1493 ft

Region	North Western
OS Grid	NY227218
Parent Peak	Outerside

Date	Weather Condition

Ascent Start Time	Peak Time	Ascent Duration

Descent Start Time	Finish Time	Descent Duration

Notes

Total Duration	Total Distance

Difficulty: [1] [2] [3] [4] [5] [6] [7] [8] [9] [10]
Views: [1] [2] [3] [4] [5] [6] [7] [8] [9] [10]

RAVEN CRAG
461 m / 1512 ft

Region	Central
OS Grid	NY303187
Parent Peak	High Seat

Date	Weather Condition

Ascent Start Time	Peak Time	Ascent Duration

Descent Start Time	Finish Time	Descent Duration

Notes	Total Duration	Total Distance

Difficulty: (1) (2) (3) (4) (5) (6) (7) (8) (9) (10)
Views: (1) (2) (3) (4) (5) (6) (7) (8) (9) (10)

BARF
469 m / 1539 ft

Region	North Western
OS Grid	NY214267
Parent Peak	Lord's Seat

Date	Weather Condition

Ascent Start Time	Peak Time	Ascent Duration

Descent Start Time	Finish Time	Descent Duration

Notes	Total Duration	Total Distance

Difficulty: (1) (2) (3) (4) (5) (6) (7) (8) (9) (10)
Views: (1) (2) (3) (4) (5) (6) (7) (8) (9) (10)

LINGMOOR FELL
470 m / 1542 ft

Region	Southern
OS Grid	NY302046
Parent Peak	Scafell Pike

Date	Weather Condition

Ascent Start Time	Peak Time	Ascent Duration

Descent Start Time	Finish Time	Descent Duration

Notes

	Total Duration	Total Distance

Difficulty: [1] [2] [3] [4] [5] [6] [7] [8] [9] [10]
Views: [1] [2] [3] [4] [5] [6] [7] [8] [9] [10]

ARMBOTH FELL
475 m / 1558 ft

Region	Central
OS Grid	NY295157
Parent Peak	High Seat

Date	Weather Condition

Ascent Start Time	Peak Time	Ascent Duration

Descent Start Time	Finish Time	Descent Duration

Notes

	Total Duration	Total Distance

Difficulty: [1] [2] [3] [4] [5] [6] [7] [8] [9] [10]
Views: [1] [2] [3] [4] [5] [6] [7] [8] [9] [10]

BURNBANK FELL
475 m / 1558 ft

Region	Western
OS Grid	NY110209
Parent Peak	Blake Fell

Date	Weather Condition

Ascent Start Time	Peak Time	Ascent Duration

Descent Start Time	Finish Time	Descent Duration

Notes	Total Duration	Total Distance

Difficulty [1] [2] [3] [4] [5] [6] [7] [8] [9] [10]
Views [1] [2] [3] [4] [5] [6] [7] [8] [9] [10]

GOWBARROW FELL
481 m / 1579 ft

Region	Eastern
OS Grid	NY407218
Parent Peak	Little Mell Fell

Date	Weather Condition

Ascent Start Time	Peak Time	Ascent Duration

Descent Start Time	Finish Time	Descent Duration

Notes	Total Duration	Total Distance

Difficulty [1] [2] [3] [4] [5] [6] [7] [8] [9] [10]
Views [1] [2] [3] [4] [5] [6] [7] [8] [9] [10]

LONGLANDS FELL
483 m / 1585 ft

Region	Northern
OS Grid	NY275354
Parent Peak	Lowthwaite Fell

Date	Weather Condition

Ascent Start Time	Peak Time	Ascent Duration

Descent Start Time	Finish Time	Descent Duration

Notes

Total Duration	Total Distance

Difficulty: 1 2 3 4 5 6 7 8 9 10
Views: 1 2 3 4 5 6 7 8 9 10

SOUR HOWES
483 m / 1585 ft

Region	Far Eastern
OS Grid	NY427032
Parent Peak	Sallows

Date	Weather Condition

Ascent Start Time	Peak Time	Ascent Duration

Descent Start Time	Finish Time	Descent Duration

Notes

Total Duration	Total Distance

Difficulty: 1 2 3 4 5 6 7 8 9 10
Views: 1 2 3 4 5 6 7 8 9 10

BAYSTONES (WANSFELL)
487 m / 1597 ft

Region	Far Eastern
OS Grid	NY403051
Parent Peak	Caudale Moor

Date	Weather Condition

Ascent Start Time	Peak Time	Ascent Duration

Descent Start Time	Finish Time	Descent Duration

Notes

Total Duration	Total Distance

Difficulty: [1] [2] [3] [4] [5] [6] [7] [8] [9] [10]
Views: [1] [2] [3] [4] [5] [6] [7] [8] [9] [10]

GRIKE
488 m / 1601 ft

Region	Western
OS Grid	NY084140
Parent Peak	Crag Fell

Date	Weather Condition

Ascent Start Time	Peak Time	Ascent Duration

Descent Start Time	Finish Time	Descent Duration

Notes

Total Duration	Total Distance

Difficulty: [1] [2] [3] [4] [5] [6] [7] [8] [9] [10]
Views: [1] [2] [3] [4] [5] [6] [7] [8] [9] [10]

GREEN CRAG
489 m / 1603 ft

Region	Southern
OS Grid	SD200982
Parent Peak	Harter Fell

Date	Weather Condition

Ascent Start Time	Peak Time	Ascent Duration

Descent Start Time	Finish Time	Descent Duration

Notes

	Total Duration	Total Distance

Difficulty	1 2 3 4 5 6 7 8 9 10
Views	1 2 3 4 5 6 7 8 9 10

DODD
502 m / 1647 ft

Region	Northern
OS Grid	NY244273
Parent Peak	Skiddaw

Date	Weather Condition

Ascent Start Time	Peak Time	Ascent Duration

Descent Start Time	Finish Time	Descent Duration

Notes

	Total Duration	Total Distance

Difficulty	1 2 3 4 5 6 7 8 9 10
Views	1 2 3 4 5 6 7 8 9 10

STONE ARTHUR
504 m / 1654 ft

Region	Eastern
OS Grid	NY347092
Parent Peak	Great Rigg

Date	Weather Condition

Ascent Start Time	Peak Time	Ascent Duration

Descent Start Time	Finish Time	Descent Duration

Notes	Total Duration	Total Distance

Difficulty [1] [2] [3] [4] [5] [6] [7] [8] [9] [10]
Views [1] [2] [3] [4] [5] [6] [7] [8] [9] [10]

LITTLE MELL FELL
505 m / 1657 ft

Region	Eastern
OS Grid	NY423240
Parent Peak	Helvellyn

Date	Weather Condition

Ascent Start Time	Peak Time	Ascent Duration

Descent Start Time	Finish Time	Descent Duration

Notes	Total Duration	Total Distance

Difficulty [1] [2] [3] [4] [5] [6] [7] [8] [9] [10]
Views [1] [2] [3] [4] [5] [6] [7] [8] [9] [10]

Low Pike
508 m / 1667 ft

Region	Eastern
OS Grid	NY373078
Parent Peak	Dove Crag

Date	Weather Condition

Ascent Start Time	Peak Time	Ascent Duration

Descent Start Time	Finish Time	Descent Duration

Notes	Total Duration	Total Distance

Difficulty: (1) (2) (3) (4) (5) (6) (7) (8) (9) (10)
Views: (1) (2) (3) (4) (5) (6) (7) (8) (9) (10)

Beda Fell (Beda Head)
509 m / 1670 ft

Region	Far Eastern
OS Grid	NY428171
Parent Peak	Angletarn Pikes

Date	Weather Condition

Ascent Start Time	Peak Time	Ascent Duration

Descent Start Time	Finish Time	Descent Duration

Notes	Total Duration	Total Distance

Difficulty: (1) (2) (3) (4) (5) (6) (7) (8) (9) (10)
Views: (1) (2) (3) (4) (5) (6) (7) (8) (9) (10)

HEN TOMB
509 m / 1670 ft

Region	Western
OS Grid	NY132181
Parent Peak	

Date	Weather Condition

Ascent Start Time	Peak Time	Ascent Duration

Descent Start Time	Finish Time	Descent Duration

Notes	Total Duration	Total Distance

Difficulty	1 2 3 4 5 6 7 8 9 10
Views	1 2 3 4 5 6 7 8 9 10

BROOM FELL
511 m / 1677 ft

Region	North Western
OS Grid	NY194271
Parent Peak	Lord's Seat

Date	Weather Condition

Ascent Start Time	Peak Time	Ascent Duration

Descent Start Time	Finish Time	Descent Duration

Notes	Total Duration	Total Distance

Difficulty	1 2 3 4 5 6 7 8 9 10
Views	1 2 3 4 5 6 7 8 9 10

MELLBREAK
512 m / 1680 ft

Region	Western
OS Grid	NY148186
Parent Peak	High Stile

Date	Weather Condition

Ascent Start Time	Peak Time	Ascent Duration

Descent Start Time	Finish Time	Descent Duration

Notes

Total Duration	Total Distance

Difficulty	1 2 3 4 5 6 7 8 9 10
Views	1 2 3 4 5 6 7 8 9 10

HIGH TOVE
515 m / 1690 ft

Region	Central
OS Grid	NY289165
Parent Peak	High Seat

Date	Weather Condition

Ascent Start Time	Peak Time	Ascent Duration

Descent Start Time	Finish Time	Descent Duration

Notes

Total Duration	Total Distance

Difficulty	1 2 3 4 5 6 7 8 9 10
Views	1 2 3 4 5 6 7 8 9 10

SALLOWS

516 m / 1693 ft

Region	Far Eastern
OS Grid	NY436039
Parent Peak	Ill Bell

Date	Weather Condition

Ascent Start Time	Peak Time	Ascent Duration

Descent Start Time	Finish Time	Descent Duration

Notes	Total Duration	Total Distance
	Difficulty	[1] [2] [3] [4] [5] [6] [7] [8] [9] [10]
	Views	[1] [2] [3] [4] [5] [6] [7] [8] [9] [10]

WHINLATTER (BROWN HOW)

517 m / 1696 ft

Region	North Western
OS Grid	NY191251
Parent Peak	Lord's Seat

Date	Weather Condition

Ascent Start Time	Peak Time	Ascent Duration

Descent Start Time	Finish Time	Descent Duration

Notes	Total Duration	Total Distance
	Difficulty	[1] [2] [3] [4] [5] [6] [7] [8] [9] [10]
	Views	[1] [2] [3] [4] [5] [6] [7] [8] [9] [10]

High Hartsop Dodd
519 m / 1703 ft

Region	Eastern
OS Grid	NY393107
Parent Peak	Little Hart Crag

Date	Weather Condition

Ascent Start Time	Peak Time	Ascent Duration

Descent Start Time	Finish Time	Descent Duration

Notes

Total Duration	Total Distance

Difficulty: [1] [2] [3] [4] [5] [6] [7] [8] [9] [10]
Views: [1] [2] [3] [4] [5] [6] [7] [8] [9] [10]

Souther Fell
522 m / 1713 ft

Region	Northern
OS Grid	NY354291
Parent Peak	Blencathra

Date	Weather Condition

Ascent Start Time	Peak Time	Ascent Duration

Descent Start Time	Finish Time	Descent Duration

Notes

Total Duration	Total Distance

Difficulty: [1] [2] [3] [4] [5] [6] [7] [8] [9] [10]
Views: [1] [2] [3] [4] [5] [6] [7] [8] [9] [10]

CRAG FELL
523 m / 1716 ft

Region	Western
OS Grid	NY097143
Parent Peak	Pillar

Date	Weather Condition

Ascent Start Time	Peak Time	Ascent Duration

Descent Start Time	Finish Time	Descent Duration

Notes	Total Duration	Total Distance

Difficulty: [1] [2] [3] [4] [5] [6] [7] [8] [9] [10]
Views: [1] [2] [3] [4] [5] [6] [7] [8] [9] [10]

BONSCALE PIKE
524 m / 1719 ft

Region	Far Eastern
OS Grid	NY453200
Parent Peak	Loadpot Hill

Date	Weather Condition

Ascent Start Time	Peak Time	Ascent Duration

Descent Start Time	Finish Time	Descent Duration

Notes	Total Duration	Total Distance

Difficulty: [1] [2] [3] [4] [5] [6] [7] [8] [9] [10]
Views: [1] [2] [3] [4] [5] [6] [7] [8] [9] [10]

EAGLE CRAG
525 m / 1722 ft

Region	Central
OS Grid	NY275121
Parent Peak	Sergeant's Crag

Date	Weather Condition

Ascent Start Time	Peak Time	Ascent Duration

Descent Start Time	Finish Time	Descent Duration

Notes	Total Duration	Total Distance

Difficulty: [1] [2] [3] [4] [5] [6] [7] [8] [9] [10]
Views: [1] [2] [3] [4] [5] [6] [7] [8] [9] [10]

GAVEL FELL
526 m / 1726 ft

Region	Western
OS Grid	NY116183
Parent Peak	Blake Fell

Date	Weather Condition

Ascent Start Time	Peak Time	Ascent Duration

Descent Start Time	Finish Time	Descent Duration

Notes	Total Duration	Total Distance

Difficulty: [1] [2] [3] [4] [5] [6] [7] [8] [9] [10]
Views: [1] [2] [3] [4] [5] [6] [7] [8] [9] [10]

GREAT COCKUP

526 m / 1726 ft

Region	Northern
OS Grid	NY273333
Parent Peak	Knott

Date	Weather Condition

Ascent Start Time	Peak Time	Ascent Duration

Descent Start Time	Finish Time	Descent Duration

Notes	Total Duration	Total Distance

Difficulty [1] [2] [3] [4] [5] [6] [7] [8] [9] [10]
Views [1] [2] [3] [4] [5] [6] [7] [8] [9] [10]

ARTHUR'S PIKE

533 m / 1749 ft

Region	Far Eastern
OS Grid	NY460206
Parent Peak	Loadpot Hill

Date	Weather Condition

Ascent Start Time	Peak Time	Ascent Duration

Descent Start Time	Finish Time	Descent Duration

Notes	Total Duration	Total Distance

Difficulty [1] [2] [3] [4] [5] [6] [7] [8] [9] [10]
Views [1] [2] [3] [4] [5] [6] [7] [8] [9] [10]

CALF CRAG

537 m / 1762 ft

Region	Central
OS Grid	NY301104
Parent Peak	High Raise

Date	Weather Condition

Ascent Start Time	Peak Time	Ascent Duration

Descent Start Time	Finish Time	Descent Duration

Notes

Total Duration	Total Distance

Difficulty: [1] [2] [3] [4] [5] [6] [7] [8] [9] [10]
Views: [1] [2] [3] [4] [5] [6] [7] [8] [9] [10]

GREAT MELL FELL

537 m / 1762 ft

Region	Eastern
OS Grid	NY396253
Parent Peak	Helvellyn

Date	Weather Condition

Ascent Start Time	Peak Time	Ascent Duration

Descent Start Time	Finish Time	Descent Duration

Notes

Total Duration	Total Distance

Difficulty: [1] [2] [3] [4] [5] [6] [7] [8] [9] [10]
Views: [1] [2] [3] [4] [5] [6] [7] [8] [9] [10]

Whin Rigg
537 m / 1762 ft

Region	Southern
OS Grid	NY151035
Parent Peak	Illgill Head

Date	Weather Condition

Ascent Start Time	Peak Time	Ascent Duration

Descent Start Time	Finish Time	Descent Duration

Notes	Total Duration	Total Distance

Difficulty: (1) (2) (3) (4) (5) (6) (7) (8) (9) (10)
Views: (1) (2) (3) (4) (5) (6) (7) (8) (9) (10)

Blea Rigg
541 m / 1775 ft

Region	Central
OS Grid	NY301078
Parent Peak	Harrison Stickle

Date	Weather Condition

Ascent Start Time	Peak Time	Ascent Duration

Descent Start Time	Finish Time	Descent Duration

Notes	Total Duration	Total Distance

Difficulty: (1) (2) (3) (4) (5) (6) (7) (8) (9) (10)
Views: (1) (2) (3) (4) (5) (6) (7) (8) (9) (10)

LANK RIGG
541 m / 1775 ft

Region	Western
OS Grid	NY091119
Parent Peak	

Date	Weather Condition

Ascent Start Time	Peak Time	Ascent Duration

Descent Start Time	Finish Time	Descent Duration

Notes

	Total Duration	Total Distance
Difficulty	1 2 3 4 5 6 7 8 9 10	
Views	1 2 3 4 5 6 7 8 9 10	

HARD KNOTT
549 m / 1801 ft

Region	Southern
OS Grid	NY231023
Parent Peak	Scafell Pike

Date	Weather Condition

Ascent Start Time	Peak Time	Ascent Duration

Descent Start Time	Finish Time	Descent Duration

Notes

	Total Duration	Total Distance
Difficulty	1 2 3 4 5 6 7 8 9 10	
Views	1 2 3 4 5 6 7 8 9 10	

Tarn Crag (Easedale)

549 m / 1801 ft

Region	Central
OS Grid	NY303093
Parent Peak	Codale Head

Date	Weather Condition

Ascent Start Time	Peak Time	Ascent Duration

Descent Start Time	Finish Time	Descent Duration

Notes

Total Duration	Total Distance

Difficulty: [1] [2] [3] [4] [5] [6] [7] [8] [9] [10]
Views: [1] [2] [3] [4] [5] [6] [7] [8] [9] [10]

Meal Fell

550 m / 1804 ft

Region	Northern
OS Grid	NY283337
Parent Peak	Knott

Date	Weather Condition

Ascent Start Time	Peak Time	Ascent Duration

Descent Start Time	Finish Time	Descent Duration

Notes

Total Duration	Total Distance

Difficulty: [1] [2] [3] [4] [5] [6] [7] [8] [9] [10]
Views: [1] [2] [3] [4] [5] [6] [7] [8] [9] [10]

Rosthwaite Fell

551 m / 1808 ft

Region	Southern
OS Grid	NY258124
Parent Peak	Dovenest Top

Date	Weather Condition

Ascent Start Time	Peak Time	Ascent Duration

Descent Start Time	Finish Time	Descent Duration

Notes	Total Duration	Total Distance

Difficulty: [1] [2] [3] [4] [5] [6] [7] [8] [9] [10]
Views: [1] [2] [3] [4] [5] [6] [7] [8] [9] [10]

Lord's Seat

552 m / 1811 ft

Region	North Western
OS Grid	NY204265
Parent Peak	Grasmoor

Date	Weather Condition

Ascent Start Time	Peak Time	Ascent Duration

Descent Start Time	Finish Time	Descent Duration

Notes	Total Duration	Total Distance

Difficulty: [1] [2] [3] [4] [5] [6] [7] [8] [9] [10]
Views: [1] [2] [3] [4] [5] [6] [7] [8] [9] [10]

Steel Fell (Dead Pike)
553 m / 1814 ft

Region	Central
OS Grid	NY319111
Parent Peak	High Raise

Date	Weather Condition

Ascent Start Time	Peak Time	Ascent Duration

Descent Start Time	Finish Time	Descent Duration

Notes

Total Duration	Total Distance

Difficulty: (1) (2) (3) (4) (5) (6) (7) (8) (9) (10)
Views: (1) (2) (3) (4) (5) (6) (7) (8) (9) (10)

Knott Rigg
556 m / 1824 ft

Region	North Western
OS Grid	NY197188
Parent Peak	Ard Crags

Date	Weather Condition

Ascent Start Time	Peak Time	Ascent Duration

Descent Start Time	Finish Time	Descent Duration

Notes

Total Duration	Total Distance

Difficulty: (1) (2) (3) (4) (5) (6) (7) (8) (9) (10)
Views: (1) (2) (3) (4) (5) (6) (7) (8) (9) (10)

BROCK CRAGS
561 m / 1841 ft

Region	Far Eastern
OS Grid	NY416136
Parent Peak	Rest Dodd

Date	Weather Condition

Ascent Start Time	Peak Time	Ascent Duration

Descent Start Time	Finish Time	Descent Duration

Notes

	Total Duration	Total Distance
Difficulty	1 2 3 4 5 6 7 8 9 10	
Views	1 2 3 4 5 6 7 8 9 10	

ANGLETARN PIKES
567 m / 1860 ft

Region	Far Eastern
OS Grid	NY413148
Parent Peak	Rest Dodd

Date	Weather Condition

Ascent Start Time	Peak Time	Ascent Duration

Descent Start Time	Finish Time	Descent Duration

Notes

	Total Duration	Total Distance
Difficulty	1 2 3 4 5 6 7 8 9 10	
Views	1 2 3 4 5 6 7 8 9 10	

OUTERSIDE
568 m / 1864 ft

Region	North Western
OS Grid	NY211214
Parent Peak	Crag Hill

Date	Weather Condition

Ascent Start Time	Peak Time	Ascent Duration

Descent Start Time	Finish Time	Descent Duration

Notes

Total Duration	Total Distance

Difficulty [1] [2] [3] [4] [5] [6] [7] [8] [9] [10]
Views [1] [2] [3] [4] [5] [6] [7] [8] [9] [10]

SERGEANT'S CRAG
571 m / 1873 ft

Region	Central
OS Grid	NY273113
Parent Peak	High Raise

Date	Weather Condition

Ascent Start Time	Peak Time	Ascent Duration

Descent Start Time	Finish Time	Descent Duration

Notes

Total Duration	Total Distance

Difficulty [1] [2] [3] [4] [5] [6] [7] [8] [9] [10]
Views [1] [2] [3] [4] [5] [6] [7] [8] [9] [10]

BLAKE FELL
573 m / 1880 ft

Region	Western
OS Grid	NY110196
Parent Peak	High Stile

Date	Weather Condition

Ascent Start Time	Peak Time	Ascent Duration

Descent Start Time	Finish Time	Descent Duration

Notes	Total Duration	Total Distance

Difficulty	(1) (2) (3) (4) (5) (6) (7) (8) (9) (10)
Views	(1) (2) (3) (4) (5) (6) (7) (8) (9) (10)

MAIDEN MOOR
575 m / 1886 ft

Region	North Western
OS Grid	NY236181
Parent Peak	High Spy

Date	Weather Condition

Ascent Start Time	Peak Time	Ascent Duration

Descent Start Time	Finish Time	Descent Duration

Notes	Total Duration	Total Distance

Difficulty	(1) (2) (3) (4) (5) (6) (7) (8) (9) (10)
Views	(1) (2) (3) (4) (5) (6) (7) (8) (9) (10)

The Nab
576 m / 1890 ft

Region	Far Eastern
OS Grid	NY434151
Parent Peak	Rest Dodd

Date	Weather Condition

Ascent Start Time	Peak Time	Ascent Duration

Descent Start Time	Finish Time	Descent Duration

Notes

Total Duration	Total Distance

Difficulty: (1) (2) (3) (4) (5) (6) (7) (8) (9) (10)
Views: (1) (2) (3) (4) (5) (6) (7) (8) (9) (10)

Ard Crags
581 m / 1906 ft

Region	North Western
OS Grid	NY206197
Parent Peak	Grasmoor

Date	Weather Condition

Ascent Start Time	Peak Time	Ascent Duration

Descent Start Time	Finish Time	Descent Duration

Notes

Total Duration	Total Distance

Difficulty: (1) (2) (3) (4) (5) (6) (7) (8) (9) (10)
Views: (1) (2) (3) (4) (5) (6) (7) (8) (9) (10)

Hartsop Above How

581 m / 1906 ft

Region	Eastern
OS Grid	NY383120
Parent Peak	Hart Crag

Date	Weather Condition

Ascent Start Time	Peak Time	Ascent Duration

Descent Start Time	Finish Time	Descent Duration

Notes

Total Duration	Total Distance

Difficulty	[1] [2] [3] [4] [5] [6] [7] [8] [9] [10]
Views	[1] [2] [3] [4] [5] [6] [7] [8] [9] [10]

Middle Fell

582 m / 1909 ft

Region	Western
OS Grid	NY150072
Parent Peak	

Date	Weather Condition

Ascent Start Time	Peak Time	Ascent Duration

Descent Start Time	Finish Time	Descent Duration

Notes

Total Duration	Total Distance

Difficulty	[1] [2] [3] [4] [5] [6] [7] [8] [9] [10]
Views	[1] [2] [3] [4] [5] [6] [7] [8] [9] [10]

BRAE FELL
586 m / 1923 ft

Region	Northern
OS Grid	NY288351
Parent Peak	Knott

Date	Weather Condition

Ascent Start Time	Peak Time	Ascent Duration

Descent Start Time	Finish Time	Descent Duration

Notes	Total Duration	Total Distance
	Difficulty	1 2 3 4 5 6 7 8 9 10
	Views	1 2 3 4 5 6 7 8 9 10

SHIPMAN KNOTTS
587 m / 1926 ft

Region	Far Eastern
OS Grid	NY472062
Parent Peak	Kentmere Pike

Date	Weather Condition

Ascent Start Time	Peak Time	Ascent Duration

Descent Start Time	Finish Time	Descent Duration

Notes	Total Duration	Total Distance
	Difficulty	1 2 3 4 5 6 7 8 9 10
	Views	1 2 3 4 5 6 7 8 9 10

Bleaberry Fell

590 m / 1936 ft

Region	Central
OS Grid	NY285195
Parent Peak	High Seat

Date	Weather Condition

Ascent Start Time	Peak Time	Ascent Duration

Descent Start Time	Finish Time	Descent Duration

Notes	Total Duration	Total Distance

Difficulty: 1 2 3 4 5 6 7 8 9 10
Views: 1 2 3 4 5 6 7 8 9 10

Haystacks (Buttermere)

597 m / 1959 ft

Region	Western
OS Grid	NY193131
Parent Peak	

Date	Weather Condition

Ascent Start Time	Peak Time	Ascent Duration

Descent Start Time	Finish Time	Descent Duration

Notes	Total Duration	Total Distance

Difficulty: 1 2 3 4 5 6 7 8 9 10
Views: 1 2 3 4 5 6 7 8 9 10

Seathwaite Fell

601 m / 1972 ft

Region	Southern
OS Grid	NY229101
Parent Peak	Great End

Date	Weather Condition

Ascent Start Time	Peak Time	Ascent Duration

Descent Start Time	Finish Time	Descent Duration

Notes

	Total Duration	Total Distance
Difficulty	1 2 3 4 5 6 7 8 9 10	
Views	1 2 3 4 5 6 7 8 9 10	

High Seat

608 m / 1995 ft

Region	Central
OS Grid	NY287180
Parent Peak	High Raise

Date	Weather Condition

Ascent Start Time	Peak Time	Ascent Duration

Descent Start Time	Finish Time	Descent Duration

Notes

	Total Duration	Total Distance
Difficulty	1 2 3 4 5 6 7 8 9 10	
Views	1 2 3 4 5 6 7 8 9 10	

ILLGILL HEAD
609 m / 1998 ft

Region	Southern
OS Grid	NY168049
Parent Peak	Scafell Pike

Date	Weather Condition

Ascent Start Time	Peak Time	Ascent Duration

Descent Start Time	Finish Time	Descent Duration

Notes	Total Duration	Total Distance

Difficulty: [1] [2] [3] [4] [5] [6] [7] [8] [9] [10]
Views: [1] [2] [3] [4] [5] [6] [7] [8] [9] [10]

HERON PIKE
612 m / 2008 ft

Region	Eastern
OS Grid	NY355083
Parent Peak	Great Rigg

Date	Weather Condition

Ascent Start Time	Peak Time	Ascent Duration

Descent Start Time	Finish Time	Descent Duration

Notes	Total Duration	Total Distance

Difficulty: [1] [2] [3] [4] [5] [6] [7] [8] [9] [10]
Views: [1] [2] [3] [4] [5] [6] [7] [8] [9] [10]

GREAT BORNE
616 m / 2021 ft

Region	Western
OS Grid	NY123163
Parent Peak	High Stile

Date	Weather Condition

Ascent Start Time	Peak Time	Ascent Duration

Descent Start Time	Finish Time	Descent Duration

Notes

Total Duration	Total Distance

Difficulty: [1] [2] [3] [4] [5] [6] [7] [8] [9] [10]
Views: [1] [2] [3] [4] [5] [6] [7] [8] [9] [10]

HARTSOP DODD
618 m / 2028 ft

Region	Far Eastern
OS Grid	NY411118
Parent Peak	Stony Cove Pike

Date	Weather Condition

Ascent Start Time	Peak Time	Ascent Duration

Descent Start Time	Finish Time	Descent Duration

Notes

Total Duration	Total Distance

Difficulty: [1] [2] [3] [4] [5] [6] [7] [8] [9] [10]
Views: [1] [2] [3] [4] [5] [6] [7] [8] [9] [10]

BIRKS
622 m / 2041 ft

Region	Eastern
OS Grid	NY380143
Parent Peak	St Sunday Crag

Date	Weather Condition

Ascent Start Time	Peak Time	Ascent Duration

Descent Start Time	Finish Time	Descent Duration

Notes

Total Duration	Total Distance

Difficulty [1] [2] [3] [4] [5] [6] [7] [8] [9] [10]
Views [1] [2] [3] [4] [5] [6] [7] [8] [9] [10]

YEWBARROW
627 m / 2057 ft

Region	Western
OS Grid	NY173084
Parent Peak	

Date	Weather Condition

Ascent Start Time	Peak Time	Ascent Duration

Descent Start Time	Finish Time	Descent Duration

Notes

Total Duration	Total Distance

Difficulty [1] [2] [3] [4] [5] [6] [7] [8] [9] [10]
Views [1] [2] [3] [4] [5] [6] [7] [8] [9] [10]

MUNGRISDALE COMMON
633 m / 2077 ft

Region	Northern
OS Grid	NY310292
Parent Peak	Atkinson Pike

Date	Weather Condition

Ascent Start Time	Peak Time	Ascent Duration

Descent Start Time	Finish Time	Descent Duration

Notes

Total Duration	Total Distance

Difficulty: 1 2 3 4 5 6 7 8 9 10
Views: 1 2 3 4 5 6 7 8 9 10

STARLING DODD
633 m / 2077 ft

Region	Western
OS Grid	NY142157
Parent Peak	

Date	Weather Condition

Ascent Start Time	Peak Time	Ascent Duration

Descent Start Time	Finish Time	Descent Duration

Notes

Total Duration	Total Distance

Difficulty: 1 2 3 4 5 6 7 8 9 10
Views: 1 2 3 4 5 6 7 8 9 10

Causey Pike

637 m / 2090 ft

Region	North Western
OS Grid	NY218208
Parent Peak	Scar Crags

Date	Weather Condition

Ascent Start Time	Peak Time	Ascent Duration

Descent Start Time	Finish Time	Descent Duration

Notes

Total Duration	Total Distance

Difficulty: 1 2 3 4 5 6 7 8 9 10
Views: 1 2 3 4 5 6 7 8 9 10

Little Hart Crag

637 m / 2090 ft

Region	Eastern
OS Grid	NY387100
Parent Peak	Dove Crag

Date	Weather Condition

Ascent Start Time	Peak Time	Ascent Duration

Descent Start Time	Finish Time	Descent Duration

Notes

Total Duration	Total Distance

Difficulty: 1 2 3 4 5 6 7 8 9 10
Views: 1 2 3 4 5 6 7 8 9 10

GREY CRAG (SLEDDALE)

638 m / 2093 ft

Region	Far Eastern
OS Grid	NY497072
Parent Peak	Tarn Crag

Date	Weather Condition

Ascent Start Time	Peak Time	Ascent Duration

Descent Start Time	Finish Time	Descent Duration

Notes	Total Duration	Total Distance

Difficulty: [1] [2] [3] [4] [5] [6] [7] [8] [9] [10]
Views: [1] [2] [3] [4] [5] [6] [7] [8] [9] [10]

BASE BROWN

646 m / 2119 ft

Region	Western
OS Grid	NY225114
Parent Peak	Green Gable

Date	Weather Condition

Ascent Start Time	Peak Time	Ascent Duration

Descent Start Time	Finish Time	Descent Duration

Notes	Total Duration	Total Distance

Difficulty: [1] [2] [3] [4] [5] [6] [7] [8] [9] [10]
Views: [1] [2] [3] [4] [5] [6] [7] [8] [9] [10]

Fleetwith Pike

649 m / 2129 ft

Region	Western
OS Grid	NY205141
Parent Peak	Great Gable

Date	Weather Condition

Ascent Start Time	Peak Time	Ascent Duration

Descent Start Time	Finish Time	Descent Duration

Notes

Total Duration	Total Distance

Difficulty: 1 2 3 4 5 6 7 8 9 10
Views: 1 2 3 4 5 6 7 8 9 10

Great Sca Fell

651 m / 2136 ft

Region	Northern
OS Grid	NY291339
Parent Peak	Knott

Date	Weather Condition

Ascent Start Time	Peak Time	Ascent Duration

Descent Start Time	Finish Time	Descent Duration

Notes

Total Duration	Total Distance

Difficulty: 1 2 3 4 5 6 7 8 9 10
Views: 1 2 3 4 5 6 7 8 9 10

ROSSETT PIKE
651 m / 2136 ft

Region	Southern
OS Grid	NY249075
Parent Peak	Bowfell

Date	Weather Condition

Ascent Start Time	Peak Time	Ascent Duration

Descent Start Time	Finish Time	Descent Duration

Notes	Total Duration	Total Distance

Difficulty: (1) (2) (3) (4) (5) (6) (7) (8) (9) (10)
Views: (1) (2) (3) (4) (5) (6) (7) (8) (9) (10)

HIGH SPY
653 m / 2143 ft

Region	North Western
OS Grid	NY234162
Parent Peak	Dale Head

Date	Weather Condition

Ascent Start Time	Peak Time	Ascent Duration

Descent Start Time	Finish Time	Descent Duration

Notes	Total Duration	Total Distance

Difficulty: (1) (2) (3) (4) (5) (6) (7) (8) (9) (10)
Views: (1) (2) (3) (4) (5) (6) (7) (8) (9) (10)

Harter Fell (Eskdale)

654 m / 2146 ft

Region	Southern
OS Grid	SD218997
Parent Peak	Scafell Pike

Date	Weather Condition

Ascent Start Time	Peak Time	Ascent Duration

Descent Start Time	Finish Time	Descent Duration

Notes

Total Duration	Total Distance

Difficulty: 1 2 3 4 5 6 7 8 9 10
Views: 1 2 3 4 5 6 7 8 9 10

Middle Dodd

654 m / 2146 ft

Region	Eastern
OS Grid	NY397095
Parent Peak	Red Screes

Date	Weather Condition

Ascent Start Time	Peak Time	Ascent Duration

Descent Start Time	Finish Time	Descent Duration

Notes

Total Duration	Total Distance

Difficulty: 1 2 3 4 5 6 7 8 9 10
Views: 1 2 3 4 5 6 7 8 9 10

Selside Pike

655 m / 2149 ft

Region	Far Eastern
OS Grid	NY490111
Parent Peak	Branstree

Date	Weather Condition

Ascent Start Time	Peak Time	Ascent Duration

Descent Start Time	Finish Time	Descent Duration

Notes	Total Duration	Total Distance

Difficulty: [1] [2] [3] [4] [5] [6] [7] [8] [9] [10]
Views: [1] [2] [3] [4] [5] [6] [7] [8] [9] [10]

High Pike (Scandale)

656 m / 2152 ft

Region	Eastern
OS Grid	NY374088
Parent Peak	Dove Crag

Date	Weather Condition

Ascent Start Time	Peak Time	Ascent Duration

Descent Start Time	Finish Time	Descent Duration

Notes	Total Duration	Total Distance

Difficulty: [1] [2] [3] [4] [5] [6] [7] [8] [9] [10]
Views: [1] [2] [3] [4] [5] [6] [7] [8] [9] [10]

PLACE FELL
657 m / 2156 ft

Region	Far Eastern
OS Grid	NY405169
Parent Peak	High Street

Date	Weather Condition

Ascent Start Time	Peak Time	Ascent Duration

Descent Start Time	Finish Time	Descent Duration

Notes

Total Duration	Total Distance

Difficulty [1] [2] [3] [4] [5] [6] [7] [8] [9] [10]
Views [1] [2] [3] [4] [5] [6] [7] [8] [9] [10]

HIGH PIKE (CALDBECK)
658 m / 2159 ft

Region	Northern
OS Grid	NY318350
Parent Peak	Knott

Date	Weather Condition

Ascent Start Time	Peak Time	Ascent Duration

Descent Start Time	Finish Time	Descent Duration

Notes

Total Duration	Total Distance

Difficulty [1] [2] [3] [4] [5] [6] [7] [8] [9] [10]
Views [1] [2] [3] [4] [5] [6] [7] [8] [9] [10]

WHITELESS PIKE
660 m / 2165 ft

Region	North Western
OS Grid	NY180189
Parent Peak	Crag Hill

Date	Weather Condition

Ascent Start Time	Peak Time	Ascent Duration

Descent Start Time	Finish Time	Descent Duration

Notes	Total Duration	Total Distance

Difficulty: (1) (2) (3) (4) (5) (6) (7) (8) (9) (10)
Views: (1) (2) (3) (4) (5) (6) (7) (8) (9) (10)

CARROCK FELL
663 m / 2175 ft

Region	Northern
OS Grid	NY341336
Parent Peak	Knott

Date	Weather Condition

Ascent Start Time	Peak Time	Ascent Duration

Descent Start Time	Finish Time	Descent Duration

Notes	Total Duration	Total Distance

Difficulty: (1) (2) (3) (4) (5) (6) (7) (8) (9) (10)
Views: (1) (2) (3) (4) (5) (6) (7) (8) (9) (10)

TARN CRAG (SLEDDALE)
664 m / 2178 ft

Region	Far Eastern
OS Grid	NY488078
Parent Peak	High Street

Date	Weather Condition

Ascent Start Time	Peak Time	Ascent Duration

Descent Start Time	Finish Time	Descent Duration

Notes

	Total Duration	Total Distance
Difficulty	1 2 3 4 5 6 7 8 9 10	
Views	1 2 3 4 5 6 7 8 9 10	

WETHER HILL
671 m / 2201 ft

Region	Far Eastern
OS Grid	NY455167
Parent Peak	High Raise

Date	Weather Condition

Ascent Start Time	Peak Time	Ascent Duration

Descent Start Time	Finish Time	Descent Duration

Notes

	Total Duration	Total Distance
Difficulty	1 2 3 4 5 6 7 8 9 10	
Views	1 2 3 4 5 6 7 8 9 10	

LOADPOT HILL
672 m / 2205 ft

Region	Far Eastern
OS Grid	NY456180
Parent Peak	High Raise

Date	Weather Condition

Ascent Start Time	Peak Time	Ascent Duration

Descent Start Time	Finish Time	Descent Duration

Notes

Total Duration	Total Distance

Difficulty	[1] [2] [3] [4] [5] [6] [7] [8] [9] [10]
Views	[1] [2] [3] [4] [5] [6] [7] [8] [9] [10]

SCAR CRAGS
672 m / 2205 ft

Region	North Western
OS Grid	NY208206
Parent Peak	Crag Hill

Date	Weather Condition

Ascent Start Time	Peak Time	Ascent Duration

Descent Start Time	Finish Time	Descent Duration

Notes

Total Duration	Total Distance

Difficulty	[1] [2] [3] [4] [5] [6] [7] [8] [9] [10]
Views	[1] [2] [3] [4] [5] [6] [7] [8] [9] [10]

Bakestall
673 m / 2208 ft

Region	Northern
OS Grid	NY266308
Parent Peak	Skiddaw

Date	Weather Condition

Ascent Start Time	Peak Time	Ascent Duration

Descent Start Time	Finish Time	Descent Duration

Notes	Total Duration	Total Distance

Difficulty: [1] [2] [3] [4] [5] [6] [7] [8] [9] [10]
Views: [1] [2] [3] [4] [5] [6] [7] [8] [9] [10]

Sheffield Pike
675 m / 2215 ft

Region	Eastern
OS Grid	NY369181
Parent Peak	Great Dodd

Date	Weather Condition

Ascent Start Time	Peak Time	Ascent Duration

Descent Start Time	Finish Time	Descent Duration

Notes	Total Duration	Total Distance

Difficulty: [1] [2] [3] [4] [5] [6] [7] [8] [9] [10]
Views: [1] [2] [3] [4] [5] [6] [7] [8] [9] [10]

LOFT CRAG

680 m / 2231 ft

Region	Central
OS Grid	NY277071
Parent Peak	Pike of Stickle

Date	Weather Condition

Ascent Start Time	Peak Time	Ascent Duration

Descent Start Time	Finish Time	Descent Duration

Notes	Total Duration	Total Distance

Difficulty	1 2 3 4 5 6 7 8 9 10
Views	1 2 3 4 5 6 7 8 9 10

BANNERDALE CRAGS

683 m / 2241 ft

Region	Northern
OS Grid	NY335290
Parent Peak	Bowscale Fell

Date	Weather Condition

Ascent Start Time	Peak Time	Ascent Duration

Descent Start Time	Finish Time	Descent Duration

Notes	Total Duration	Total Distance

Difficulty	1 2 3 4 5 6 7 8 9 10
Views	1 2 3 4 5 6 7 8 9 10

GREAT CALVA
690 m / 2264 ft

Region	Northern
OS Grid	NY290311
Parent Peak	Knott

Date	Weather Condition

Ascent Start Time	Peak Time	Ascent Duration

Descent Start Time	Finish Time	Descent Duration

Notes

	Total Duration	Total Distance

Difficulty: [1] [2] [3] [4] [5] [6] [7] [8] [9] [10]
Views: [1] [2] [3] [4] [5] [6] [7] [8] [9] [10]

ULLOCK PIKE
690 m / 2264 ft

Region	Northern
OS Grid	NY244287
Parent Peak	Long Side

Date	Weather Condition

Ascent Start Time	Peak Time	Ascent Duration

Descent Start Time	Finish Time	Descent Duration

Notes

	Total Duration	Total Distance

Difficulty: [1] [2] [3] [4] [5] [6] [7] [8] [9] [10]
Views: [1] [2] [3] [4] [5] [6] [7] [8] [9] [10]

SEATALLAN
692 m / 2270 ft

Region	Western
OS Grid	NY140084
Parent Peak	Pillar

Date	Weather Condition

Ascent Start Time	Peak Time	Ascent Duration

Descent Start Time	Finish Time	Descent Duration

Notes	Total Duration	Total Distance

Difficulty [1] [2] [3] [4] [5] [6] [7] [8] [9] [10]
Views [1] [2] [3] [4] [5] [6] [7] [8] [9] [10]

REST DODD
696 m / 2283 ft

Region	Far Eastern
OS Grid	NY432136
Parent Peak	High Street

Date	Weather Condition

Ascent Start Time	Peak Time	Ascent Duration

Descent Start Time	Finish Time	Descent Duration

Notes	Total Duration	Total Distance

Difficulty [1] [2] [3] [4] [5] [6] [7] [8] [9] [10]
Views [1] [2] [3] [4] [5] [6] [7] [8] [9] [10]

CAW FELL
697 m / 2287 ft

Region	Western
OS Grid	NY132109
Parent Peak	Haycock

Date	Weather Condition

Ascent Start Time	Peak Time	Ascent Duration

Descent Start Time	Finish Time	Descent Duration

Notes

Total Duration	Total Distance

Difficulty 1 2 3 4 5 6 7 8 9 10
Views 1 2 3 4 5 6 7 8 9 10

GREY KNOTTS
697 m / 2287 ft

Region	Western
OS Grid	NY217125
Parent Peak	Brandreth

Date	Weather Condition

Ascent Start Time	Peak Time	Ascent Duration

Descent Start Time	Finish Time	Descent Duration

Notes

Total Duration	Total Distance

Difficulty 1 2 3 4 5 6 7 8 9 10
Views 1 2 3 4 5 6 7 8 9 10

Gray Crag
699 m / 2293 ft

Region	Far Eastern
OS Grid	NY427117
Parent Peak	Thornthwaite Crag

Date	Weather Condition

Ascent Start Time	Peak Time	Ascent Duration

Descent Start Time	Finish Time	Descent Duration

Notes	Total Duration	Total Distance

Difficulty: [1] [2] [3] [4] [5] [6] [7] [8] [9] [10]
Views: [1] [2] [3] [4] [5] [6] [7] [8] [9] [10]

Pavey Ark
700 m / 2297 ft

Region	Central
OS Grid	NY284079
Parent Peak	Thunacar Knott

Date	Weather Condition

Ascent Start Time	Peak Time	Ascent Duration

Descent Start Time	Finish Time	Descent Duration

Notes	Total Duration	Total Distance

Difficulty: [1] [2] [3] [4] [5] [6] [7] [8] [9] [10]
Views: [1] [2] [3] [4] [5] [6] [7] [8] [9] [10]

COLD PIKE
701 m / 2300 ft

Region	Southern
OS Grid	NY262036
Parent Peak	Crinkle Crags

Date	Weather Condition

Ascent Start Time	Peak Time	Ascent Duration

Descent Start Time	Finish Time	Descent Duration

Notes

Total Duration	Total Distance

Difficulty: [1] [2] [3] [4] [5] [6] [7] [8] [9] [10]
Views: [1] [2] [3] [4] [5] [6] [7] [8] [9] [10]

BOWSCALE FELL
702 m / 2303 ft

Region	Northern
OS Grid	NY333305
Parent Peak	Blencathra

Date	Weather Condition

Ascent Start Time	Peak Time	Ascent Duration

Descent Start Time	Finish Time	Descent Duration

Notes

Total Duration	Total Distance

Difficulty: [1] [2] [3] [4] [5] [6] [7] [8] [9] [10]
Views: [1] [2] [3] [4] [5] [6] [7] [8] [9] [10]

PIKE OF BLISCO
705 m / 2313 ft

Region	Southern
OS Grid	NY271042
Parent Peak	Scafell Pike

Date	Weather Condition

Ascent Start Time	Peak Time	Ascent Duration

Descent Start Time	Finish Time	Descent Duration

Notes	Total Duration	Total Distance

Difficulty: [1] [2] [3] [4] [5] [6] [7] [8] [9] [10]
Views: [1] [2] [3] [4] [5] [6] [7] [8] [9] [10]

YOKE
706 m / 2316 ft

Region	Far Eastern
OS Grid	NY437067
Parent Peak	Ill Bell

Date	Weather Condition

Ascent Start Time	Peak Time	Ascent Duration

Descent Start Time	Finish Time	Descent Duration

Notes	Total Duration	Total Distance

Difficulty: [1] [2] [3] [4] [5] [6] [7] [8] [9] [10]
Views: [1] [2] [3] [4] [5] [6] [7] [8] [9] [10]

WHITESIDE (WEST TOP)
707 m / 2320 ft

Region	North Western
OS Grid	NY170219
Parent Peak	Hopegill Head

Date	Weather Condition

Ascent Start Time	Peak Time	Ascent Duration

Descent Start Time	Finish Time	Descent Duration

Notes

Total Duration	Total Distance

Difficulty: 1 2 3 4 5 6 7 8 9 10
Views: 1 2 3 4 5 6 7 8 9 10

PIKE OF STICKLE
709 m / 2326 ft

Region	Central
OS Grid	NY273073
Parent Peak	High Raise

Date	Weather Condition

Ascent Start Time	Peak Time	Ascent Duration

Descent Start Time	Finish Time	Descent Duration

Notes

Total Duration	Total Distance

Difficulty: 1 2 3 4 5 6 7 8 9 10
Views: 1 2 3 4 5 6 7 8 9 10

KNOTT
710 m / 2329 ft

Region	Northern
OS Grid	NY296329
Parent Peak	Skiddaw

Date	Weather Condition

Ascent Start Time	Peak Time	Ascent Duration

Descent Start Time	Finish Time	Descent Duration

Notes

Total Duration	Total Distance

Difficulty: [1] [2] [3] [4] [5] [6] [7] [8] [9] [10]
Views: [1] [2] [3] [4] [5] [6] [7] [8] [9] [10]

BRANSTREE
713 m / 2339 ft

Region	Far Eastern
OS Grid	NY478099
Parent Peak	Harter Fell

Date	Weather Condition

Ascent Start Time	Peak Time	Ascent Duration

Descent Start Time	Finish Time	Descent Duration

Notes

Total Duration	Total Distance

Difficulty: [1] [2] [3] [4] [5] [6] [7] [8] [9] [10]
Views: [1] [2] [3] [4] [5] [6] [7] [8] [9] [10]

BRANDRETH
715 m / 2346 ft

Region	Western
OS Grid	NY214119
Parent Peak	Great Gable

Date	Weather Condition

Ascent Start Time	Peak Time	Ascent Duration

Descent Start Time	Finish Time	Descent Duration

Notes

Total Duration	Total Distance

Difficulty	[1] [2] [3] [4] [5] [6] [7] [8] [9] [10]
Views	[1] [2] [3] [4] [5] [6] [7] [8] [9] [10]

LONSCALE FELL
715 m / 2346 ft

Region	Northern
OS Grid	NY285271
Parent Peak	Skiddaw Little Man

Date	Weather Condition

Ascent Start Time	Peak Time	Ascent Duration

Descent Start Time	Finish Time	Descent Duration

Notes

Total Duration	Total Distance

Difficulty	[1] [2] [3] [4] [5] [6] [7] [8] [9] [10]
Views	[1] [2] [3] [4] [5] [6] [7] [8] [9] [10]

Birkhouse Moor

718 m / 2356 ft

Region	Eastern
OS Grid	NY363159
Parent Peak	Helvellyn

Date	Weather Condition

Ascent Start Time	Peak Time	Ascent Duration

Descent Start Time	Finish Time	Descent Duration

Notes

Total Duration	Total Distance

Difficulty	1 2 3 4 5 6 7 8 9 10
Views	1 2 3 4 5 6 7 8 9 10

Froswick

720 m / 2362 ft

Region	Far Eastern
OS Grid	NY435085
Parent Peak	Ill Bell

Date	Weather Condition

Ascent Start Time	Peak Time	Ascent Duration

Descent Start Time	Finish Time	Descent Duration

Notes

Total Duration	Total Distance

Difficulty	1 2 3 4 5 6 7 8 9 10
Views	1 2 3 4 5 6 7 8 9 10

Thunacar Knott

723 m / 2372 ft

Region	Central
OS Grid	NY279079
Parent Peak	Harrison Stickle

Date	Weather Condition

Ascent Start Time	Peak Time	Ascent Duration

Descent Start Time	Finish Time	Descent Duration

Notes

	Total Duration	Total Distance

Difficulty: [1] [2] [3] [4] [5] [6] [7] [8] [9] [10]

Views: [1] [2] [3] [4] [5] [6] [7] [8] [9] [10]

Clough Head

726 m / 2382 ft

Region	Eastern
OS Grid	NY333225
Parent Peak	Great Dodd

Date	Weather Condition

Ascent Start Time	Peak Time	Ascent Duration

Descent Start Time	Finish Time	Descent Duration

Notes

	Total Duration	Total Distance

Difficulty: [1] [2] [3] [4] [5] [6] [7] [8] [9] [10]

Views: [1] [2] [3] [4] [5] [6] [7] [8] [9] [10]

ULLSCARF

726 m / 2382 ft

Region	Central
OS Grid	NY291121
Parent Peak	High Raise

Date	Weather Condition

Ascent Start Time	Peak Time	Ascent Duration

Descent Start Time	Finish Time	Descent Duration

Notes	Total Duration	Total Distance

Difficulty: (1) (2) (3) (4) (5) (6) (7) (8) (9) (10)
Views: (1) (2) (3) (4) (5) (6) (7) (8) (9) (10)

HINDSCARTH

727 m / 2385 ft

Region	North Western
OS Grid	NY215165
Parent Peak	Dale Head

Date	Weather Condition

Ascent Start Time	Peak Time	Ascent Duration

Descent Start Time	Finish Time	Descent Duration

Notes	Total Duration	Total Distance

Difficulty: (1) (2) (3) (4) (5) (6) (7) (8) (9) (10)
Views: (1) (2) (3) (4) (5) (6) (7) (8) (9) (10)

KENTMERE PIKE
730 m / 2395 ft

Region	Far Eastern
OS Grid	NY465077
Parent Peak	Harter Fell

Date | **Weather Condition**

Ascent Start Time | **Peak Time** | **Ascent Duration**

Descent Start Time | **Finish Time** | **Descent Duration**

Notes | **Total Duration** | **Total Distance**

Difficulty: [1] [2] [3] [4] [5] [6] [7] [8] [9] [10]
Views: [1] [2] [3] [4] [5] [6] [7] [8] [9] [10]

LONG SIDE
734 m / 2408 ft

Region	Northern
OS Grid	NY248284
Parent Peak	Skiddaw

Date | **Weather Condition**

Ascent Start Time | **Peak Time** | **Ascent Duration**

Descent Start Time | **Finish Time** | **Descent Duration**

Notes | **Total Duration** | **Total Distance**

Difficulty: [1] [2] [3] [4] [5] [6] [7] [8] [9] [10]
Views: [1] [2] [3] [4] [5] [6] [7] [8] [9] [10]

Harrison Stickle

736 m / 2415 ft

Region	Central
OS Grid	NY281074
Parent Peak	High Raise

Date	Weather Condition

Ascent Start Time	Peak Time	Ascent Duration

Descent Start Time	Finish Time	Descent Duration

Notes	Total Duration	Total Distance

Difficulty: [1] [2] [3] [4] [5] [6] [7] [8] [9] [10]
Views: [1] [2] [3] [4] [5] [6] [7] [8] [9] [10]

Sergeant Man

736 m / 2415 ft

Region	Central
OS Grid	NY286088
Parent Peak	High Raise

Date	Weather Condition

Ascent Start Time	Peak Time	Ascent Duration

Descent Start Time	Finish Time	Descent Duration

Notes	Total Duration	Total Distance

Difficulty: [1] [2] [3] [4] [5] [6] [7] [8] [9] [10]
Views: [1] [2] [3] [4] [5] [6] [7] [8] [9] [10]

ROBINSON
737 m / 2418 ft

Region	**North Western**
OS Grid	**NY201168**
Parent Peak	**Dale Head**

Date	Weather Condition

Ascent Start Time	Peak Time	Ascent Duration

Descent Start Time	Finish Time	Descent Duration

Notes

Total Duration	Total Distance

Difficulty: 1 2 3 4 5 6 7 8 9 10
Views: 1 2 3 4 5 6 7 8 9 10

SEAT SANDAL
737 m / 2417 ft

Region	**Eastern**
OS Grid	**NY344115**
Parent Peak	**Fairfield**

Date	Weather Condition

Ascent Start Time	Peak Time	Ascent Duration

Descent Start Time	Finish Time	Descent Duration

Notes

Total Duration	Total Distance

Difficulty: 1 2 3 4 5 6 7 8 9 10
Views: 1 2 3 4 5 6 7 8 9 10

THE KNOTT (HIGH STREET)

739 m / 2425 ft

Region	Far Eastern
OS Grid	NY437126
Parent Peak	Rampsgill Head

Date	Weather Condition

Ascent Start Time	Peak Time	Ascent Duration

Descent Start Time	Finish Time	Descent Duration

Notes	Total Duration	Total Distance

Difficulty [1] [2] [3] [4] [5] [6] [7] [8] [9] [10]
Views [1] [2] [3] [4] [5] [6] [7] [8] [9] [10]

HIGH CRAG (BUTTERMERE)

744 m / 2441 ft

Region	Western
OS Grid	NY180139
Parent Peak	

Date	Weather Condition

Ascent Start Time	Peak Time	Ascent Duration

Descent Start Time	Finish Time	Descent Duration

Notes	Total Duration	Total Distance

Difficulty [1] [2] [3] [4] [5] [6] [7] [8] [9] [10]
Views [1] [2] [3] [4] [5] [6] [7] [8] [9] [10]

Tarl Side

746 m / 2448 ft

Region	Northern
OS Grid	NY254280
Parent Peak	Skiddaw

Date	Weather Condition

Ascent Start Time	Peak Time	Ascent Duration

Descent Start Time	Finish Time	Descent Duration

Notes

	Total Duration	Total Distance
Difficulty	1 2 3 4 5 6 7 8 9 10	
Views	1 2 3 4 5 6 7 8 9 10	

Dale Head

753 m / 2470 ft

Region	North Western
OS Grid	NY222153
Parent Peak	Great Gable

Date	Weather Condition

Ascent Start Time	Peak Time	Ascent Duration

Descent Start Time	Finish Time	Descent Duration

Notes

	Total Duration	Total Distance
Difficulty	1 2 3 4 5 6 7 8 9 10	
Views	1 2 3 4 5 6 7 8 9 10	

Red Pike (Buttermere)

755 m / 2477 ft

Region	Western
OS Grid	NY160154
Parent Peak	

Date	Weather Condition

Ascent Start Time	Peak Time	Ascent Duration

Descent Start Time	Finish Time	Descent Duration

Notes

Total Duration	Total Distance

Difficulty: 1 2 3 4 5 6 7 8 9 10
Views: 1 2 3 4 5 6 7 8 9 10

Hart Side

756 m / 2480 ft

Region	Eastern
OS Grid	NY359197
Parent Peak	Green Side

Date	Weather Condition

Ascent Start Time	Peak Time	Ascent Duration

Descent Start Time	Finish Time	Descent Duration

Notes

Total Duration	Total Distance

Difficulty: 1 2 3 4 5 6 7 8 9 10
Views: 1 2 3 4 5 6 7 8 9 10

ILL BELL
757 m / 2484 ft

Region	Far Eastern
OS Grid	NY436077
Parent Peak	High Street

Date | **Weather Condition**

Ascent Start Time | **Peak Time** | **Ascent Duration**

Descent Start Time | **Finish Time** | **Descent Duration**

Notes | **Total Duration** | **Total Distance**

Difficulty [1] [2] [3] [4] [5] [6] [7] [8] [9] [10]
Views [1] [2] [3] [4] [5] [6] [7] [8] [9] [10]

MARDALE ILL BELL
760 m / 2493 ft

Region	Far Eastern
OS Grid	NY447101
Parent Peak	High Street

Date | **Weather Condition**

Ascent Start Time | **Peak Time** | **Ascent Duration**

Descent Start Time | **Finish Time** | **Descent Duration**

Notes | **Total Duration** | **Total Distance**

Difficulty [1] [2] [3] [4] [5] [6] [7] [8] [9] [10]
Views [1] [2] [3] [4] [5] [6] [7] [8] [9] [10]

HIGH RAISE (LANGDALE)
762 m / 2500 ft

Region	Central
OS Grid	NY280095
Parent Peak	Scafell Pike

Date	Weather Condition

Ascent Start Time	Peak Time	Ascent Duration

Descent Start Time	Finish Time	Descent Duration

Notes	Total Duration	Total Distance

Difficulty	1 2 3 4 5 6 7 8 9 10
Views	1 2 3 4 5 6 7 8 9 10

SLIGHT SIDE
762 m / 2500 ft

Region	Southern
OS Grid	NY209050
Parent Peak	Sca Fell

Date	Weather Condition

Ascent Start Time	Peak Time	Ascent Duration

Descent Start Time	Finish Time	Descent Duration

Notes	Total Duration	Total Distance

Difficulty	1 2 3 4 5 6 7 8 9 10
Views	1 2 3 4 5 6 7 8 9 10

STONY COVE PIKE
763 m / 2503 ft

Region	Far Eastern
OS Grid	NY417100
Parent Peak	High Street

Date	Weather Condition

Ascent Start Time	Peak Time	Ascent Duration

Descent Start Time	Finish Time	Descent Duration

Notes

	Total Duration	Total Distance

Difficulty	1 2 3 4 5 6 7 8 9 10
Views	1 2 3 4 5 6 7 8 9 10

WETHERLAM
763 m / 2503 ft

Region	Southern
OS Grid	NY288011
Parent Peak	Coniston Old Man

Date	Weather Condition

Ascent Start Time	Peak Time	Ascent Duration

Descent Start Time	Finish Time	Descent Duration

Notes

	Total Duration	Total Distance

Difficulty	1 2 3 4 5 6 7 8 9 10
Views	1 2 3 4 5 6 7 8 9 10

GREAT RIGG
766 m / 2513 ft

Region	Eastern
OS Grid	NY355104
Parent Peak	Fairfield

Date	Weather Condition

Ascent Start Time	Peak Time	Ascent Duration

Descent Start Time	Finish Time	Descent Duration

Notes

	Total Duration	Total Distance

Difficulty: (1) (2) (3) (4) (5) (6) (7) (8) (9) (10)
Views: (1) (2) (3) (4) (5) (6) (7) (8) (9) (10)

HOPEGILL HEAD
770 m / 2526 ft

Region	North Western
OS Grid	NY185221
Parent Peak	Grisedale Pike

Date	Weather Condition

Ascent Start Time	Peak Time	Ascent Duration

Descent Start Time	Finish Time	Descent Duration

Notes

	Total Duration	Total Distance

Difficulty: (1) (2) (3) (4) (5) (6) (7) (8) (9) (10)
Views: (1) (2) (3) (4) (5) (6) (7) (8) (9) (10)

WANDOPE

772 m / 2533 ft

Region	North Western
OS Grid	NY188197
Parent Peak	Crag Hill

Date	Weather Condition

Ascent Start Time	Peak Time	Ascent Duration

Descent Start Time	Finish Time	Descent Duration

Notes

Total Duration	Total Distance

Difficulty: ① ② ③ ④ ⑤ ⑥ ⑦ ⑧ ⑨ ⑩
Views: ① ② ③ ④ ⑤ ⑥ ⑦ ⑧ ⑨ ⑩

GREY FRIAR

773 m / 2536 ft

Region	Southern
OS Grid	NY260003
Parent Peak	Swirl How

Date	Weather Condition

Ascent Start Time	Peak Time	Ascent Duration

Descent Start Time	Finish Time	Descent Duration

Notes

Total Duration	Total Distance

Difficulty: ① ② ③ ④ ⑤ ⑥ ⑦ ⑧ ⑨ ⑩
Views: ① ② ③ ④ ⑤ ⑥ ⑦ ⑧ ⑨ ⑩

SAIL
773 m / 2536 ft

Region	North Western
OS Grid	NY198202
Parent Peak	Crag Hill

Date	Weather Condition

Ascent Start Time	Peak Time	Ascent Duration

Descent Start Time	Finish Time	Descent Duration

Notes	Total Duration	Total Distance

Difficulty: 1 2 3 4 5 6 7 8 9 10
Views: 1 2 3 4 5 6 7 8 9 10

RED SCREES
776 m / 2546 ft

Region	Eastern
OS Grid	NY396087
Parent Peak	Fairfield

Date	Weather Condition

Ascent Start Time	Peak Time	Ascent Duration

Descent Start Time	Finish Time	Descent Duration

Notes	Total Duration	Total Distance

Difficulty: 1 2 3 4 5 6 7 8 9 10
Views: 1 2 3 4 5 6 7 8 9 10

Dow Crag
778 m / 2552 ft

Region	Southern
OS Grid	SD262977
Parent Peak	Coniston Old Man

Date	Weather Condition

Ascent Start Time	Peak Time	Ascent Duration

Descent Start Time	Finish Time	Descent Duration

Notes

	Total Duration	Total Distance
Difficulty	1 2 3 4 5 6 7 8 9 10	
Views	1 2 3 4 5 6 7 8 9 10	

Harter Fell (Mardale)
779 m / 2556 ft

Region	Far Eastern
OS Grid	NY459093
Parent Peak	High Street

Date	Weather Condition

Ascent Start Time	Peak Time	Ascent Duration

Descent Start Time	Finish Time	Descent Duration

Notes

	Total Duration	Total Distance
Difficulty	1 2 3 4 5 6 7 8 9 10	
Views	1 2 3 4 5 6 7 8 9 10	

KIDSTY PIKE
780 m / 2559 ft

Region	Far Eastern
OS Grid	NY447125
Parent Peak	Rampsgill Head

Date	Weather Condition

Ascent Start Time	Peak Time	Ascent Duration

Descent Start Time	Finish Time	Descent Duration

Notes	Total Duration	Total Distance

Difficulty: 1 2 3 4 5 6 7 8 9 10
Views: 1 2 3 4 5 6 7 8 9 10

GLARAMARA
783 m / 2569 ft

Region	Southern
OS Grid	NY245104
Parent Peak	Scafell Pike

Date	Weather Condition

Ascent Start Time	Peak Time	Ascent Duration

Descent Start Time	Finish Time	Descent Duration

Notes	Total Duration	Total Distance

Difficulty: 1 2 3 4 5 6 7 8 9 10
Views: 1 2 3 4 5 6 7 8 9 10

Thornthwaite Crag

784 m / 2572 ft

Region	Far Eastern
OS Grid	NY431100
Parent Peak	High Street

Date	Weather Condition

Ascent Start Time	Peak Time	Ascent Duration

Descent Start Time	Finish Time	Descent Duration

Notes

Total Duration	Total Distance

Difficulty: [1] [2] [3] [4] [5] [6] [7] [8] [9] [10]
Views: [1] [2] [3] [4] [5] [6] [7] [8] [9] [10]

Allen Crags

785 m / 2575 ft

Region	Southern
OS Grid	NY236085
Parent Peak	Scafell Pike

Date	Weather Condition

Ascent Start Time	Peak Time	Ascent Duration

Descent Start Time	Finish Time	Descent Duration

Notes

Total Duration	Total Distance

Difficulty: [1] [2] [3] [4] [5] [6] [7] [8] [9] [10]
Views: [1] [2] [3] [4] [5] [6] [7] [8] [9] [10]

GREAT TARRS

785 m / 2575 ft

Region	Southern
OS Grid	NY270009
Parent Peak	Swirl How

Date	Weather Condition

Ascent Start Time	Peak Time	Ascent Duration

Descent Start Time	Finish Time	Descent Duration

Notes	Total Duration	Total Distance

Difficulty: [1] [2] [3] [4] [5] [6] [7] [8] [9] [10]
Views: [1] [2] [3] [4] [5] [6] [7] [8] [9] [10]

WATSON'S DODD

789 m / 2589 ft

Region	Eastern
OS Grid	NY335195
Parent Peak	Great Dodd

Date	Weather Condition

Ascent Start Time	Peak Time	Ascent Duration

Descent Start Time	Finish Time	Descent Duration

Notes	Total Duration	Total Distance

Difficulty: [1] [2] [3] [4] [5] [6] [7] [8] [9] [10]
Views: [1] [2] [3] [4] [5] [6] [7] [8] [9] [10]

GRISEDALE PIKE
791 m / 2595 ft

Region	North Western
OS Grid	NY198225
Parent Peak	Grasmoor

Date	Weather Condition

Ascent Start Time	Peak Time	Ascent Duration

Descent Start Time	Finish Time	Descent Duration

Notes

Total Duration	Total Distance

Difficulty	1 2 3 4 5 6 7 8 9 10
Views	1 2 3 4 5 6 7 8 9 10

DOVE CRAG
792 m / 2598 ft

Region	Eastern
OS Grid	NY374104
Parent Peak	Hart Crag

Date	Weather Condition

Ascent Start Time	Peak Time	Ascent Duration

Descent Start Time	Finish Time	Descent Duration

Notes

Total Duration	Total Distance

Difficulty	1 2 3 4 5 6 7 8 9 10
Views	1 2 3 4 5 6 7 8 9 10

Rampsgill Head

792 m / 2598 ft

Region	Far Eastern
OS Grid	NY443128
Parent Peak	High Raise

Date	Weather Condition

Ascent Start Time	Peak Time	Ascent Duration

Descent Start Time	Finish Time	Descent Duration

Notes

Total Duration	Total Distance

Difficulty: 1 2 3 4 5 6 7 8 9 10
Views: 1 2 3 4 5 6 7 8 9 10

Brim Fell

796 m / 2612 ft

Region	Southern
OS Grid	SD270985
Parent Peak	Coniston Old Man

Date	Weather Condition

Ascent Start Time	Peak Time	Ascent Duration

Descent Start Time	Finish Time	Descent Duration

Notes

Total Duration	Total Distance

Difficulty: 1 2 3 4 5 6 7 8 9 10
Views: 1 2 3 4 5 6 7 8 9 10

HAYCOCK
797 m / 2615 ft

Region	Western
OS Grid	NY144107
Parent Peak	Pillar

Date	Weather Condition

Ascent Start Time	Peak Time	Ascent Duration

Descent Start Time	Finish Time	Descent Duration

Notes

Total Duration	Total Distance

Difficulty 1 2 3 4 5 6 7 8 9 10
Views 1 2 3 4 5 6 7 8 9 10

GREEN GABLE
801 m / 2628 ft

Region	Western
OS Grid	NY214107
Parent Peak	Great Gable

Date	Weather Condition

Ascent Start Time	Peak Time	Ascent Duration

Descent Start Time	Finish Time	Descent Duration

Notes

Total Duration	Total Distance

Difficulty 1 2 3 4 5 6 7 8 9 10
Views 1 2 3 4 5 6 7 8 9 10

HIGH RAISE (HIGH STREET)

802 m / 2631 ft

Region	Far Eastern
OS Grid	NY448134
Parent Peak	High Street

Date	Weather Condition

Ascent Start Time	Peak Time	Ascent Duration

Descent Start Time	Finish Time	Descent Duration

Notes	Total Duration	Total Distance

Difficulty: [1] [2] [3] [4] [5] [6] [7] [8] [9] [10]
Views: [1] [2] [3] [4] [5] [6] [7] [8] [9] [10]

KIRK FELL

802 m / 2631 ft

Region	Western
OS Grid	NY194104
Parent Peak	Great Gable

Date	Weather Condition

Ascent Start Time	Peak Time	Ascent Duration

Descent Start Time	Finish Time	Descent Duration

Notes	Total Duration	Total Distance

Difficulty: [1] [2] [3] [4] [5] [6] [7] [8] [9] [10]
Views: [1] [2] [3] [4] [5] [6] [7] [8] [9] [10]

Swirl How

802 m / 2633 ft

Region	Southern
OS Grid	NY272005
Parent Peak	

Date	Weather Condition

Ascent Start Time	Peak Time	Ascent Duration

Descent Start Time	Finish Time	Descent Duration

Notes

Total Duration	Total Distance

Difficulty [1] [2] [3] [4] [5] [6] [7] [8] [9] [10]
Views   [1] [2] [3] [4] [5] [6] [7] [8] [9] [10]

The Old Man of Coniston

802 m / 2633 ft

Region	Southern
OS Grid	SD272978
Parent Peak	

Date	Weather Condition

Ascent Start Time	Peak Time	Ascent Duration

Descent Start Time	Finish Time	Descent Duration

Notes

Total Duration	Total Distance

Difficulty [1] [2] [3] [4] [5] [6] [7] [8] [9] [10]
Views   [1] [2] [3] [4] [5] [6] [7] [8] [9] [10]

HIGH STILE
806 m / 2644 ft

Region	Western
OS Grid	NY167147
Parent Peak	Great Gable

Date	Weather Condition

Ascent Start Time	Peak Time	Ascent Duration

Descent Start Time	Finish Time	Descent Duration

Notes	Total Duration	Total Distance

Difficulty: (1) (2) (3) (4) (5) (6) (7) (8) (9) (10)
Views: (1) (2) (3) (4) (5) (6) (7) (8) (9) (10)

LINGMELL
807 m / 2648 ft

Region	Southern
OS Grid	NY209081
Parent Peak	Scafell Pike

Date	Weather Condition

Ascent Start Time	Peak Time	Ascent Duration

Descent Start Time	Finish Time	Descent Duration

Notes	Total Duration	Total Distance

Difficulty: (1) (2) (3) (4) (5) (6) (7) (8) (9) (10)
Views: (1) (2) (3) (4) (5) (6) (7) (8) (9) (10)

STEEPLE
819 m / 2687 ft

Region	Western
OS Grid	NY157116
Parent Peak	

Date	Weather Condition

Ascent Start Time	Peak Time	Ascent Duration

Descent Start Time	Finish Time	Descent Duration

Notes

Total Duration	Total Distance

Difficulty: ① ② ③ ④ ⑤ ⑥ ⑦ ⑧ ⑨ ⑩
Views: ① ② ③ ④ ⑤ ⑥ ⑦ ⑧ ⑨ ⑩

HART CRAG
822 m / 2697 ft

Region	Eastern
OS Grid	NY369112
Parent Peak	Fairfield

Date	Weather Condition

Ascent Start Time	Peak Time	Ascent Duration

Descent Start Time	Finish Time	Descent Duration

Notes

Total Duration	Total Distance

Difficulty: ① ② ③ ④ ⑤ ⑥ ⑦ ⑧ ⑨ ⑩
Views: ① ② ③ ④ ⑤ ⑥ ⑦ ⑧ ⑨ ⑩

RED PIKE (WASDALE)
826 m / 2710 ft

Region	Western
OS Grid	NY165106
Parent Peak	

Date	Weather Condition

Ascent Start Time	Peak Time	Ascent Duration

Descent Start Time	Finish Time	Descent Duration

Notes	Total Duration	Total Distance

Difficulty [1] [2] [3] [4] [5] [6] [7] [8] [9] [10]
Views   [1] [2] [3] [4] [5] [6] [7] [8] [9] [10]

HIGH STREET
828 m / 2717 ft

Region	Far Eastern
OS Grid	NY440110
Parent Peak	Helvellyn

Date	Weather Condition

Ascent Start Time	Peak Time	Ascent Duration

Descent Start Time	Finish Time	Descent Duration

Notes	Total Duration	Total Distance

Difficulty [1] [2] [3] [4] [5] [6] [7] [8] [9] [10]
Views   [1] [2] [3] [4] [5] [6] [7] [8] [9] [10]

Crag Hill (Eel Crag)
839 m / 2753 ft

Region	North Western
OS Grid	NY192203
Parent Peak	Grasmoor

Date	Weather Condition

Ascent Start Time	Peak Time	Ascent Duration

Descent Start Time	Finish Time	Descent Duration

Notes	Total Duration	Total Distance

Difficulty: 1 2 3 4 5 6 7 8 9 10
Views: 1 2 3 4 5 6 7 8 9 10

Scoat Fell
841 m / 2759 ft

Region	Western
OS Grid	NY159113
Parent Peak	Pillar

Date	Weather Condition

Ascent Start Time	Peak Time	Ascent Duration

Descent Start Time	Finish Time	Descent Duration

Notes	Total Duration	Total Distance

Difficulty: 1 2 3 4 5 6 7 8 9 10
Views: 1 2 3 4 5 6 7 8 9 10

St Sunday Crag

841 m / 2759 ft

Region	Eastern
OS Grid	NY369133
Parent Peak	Fairfield

Date	Weather Condition

Ascent Start Time	Peak Time	Ascent Duration

Descent Start Time	Finish Time	Descent Duration

Notes

Total Duration	Total Distance

Difficulty: 1 2 3 4 5 6 7 8 9 10
Views: 1 2 3 4 5 6 7 8 9 10

Stybarrow Dodd

843 m / 2766 ft

Region	Eastern
OS Grid	NY343189
Parent Peak	Great Dodd

Date	Weather Condition

Ascent Start Time	Peak Time	Ascent Duration

Descent Start Time	Finish Time	Descent Duration

Notes

Total Duration	Total Distance

Difficulty: 1 2 3 4 5 6 7 8 9 10
Views: 1 2 3 4 5 6 7 8 9 10

Page | 103

GRASMOOR
852 m / 2795 ft

Region	North Western
OS Grid	NY174203
Parent Peak	Scafell Pike

Date	Weather Condition

Ascent Start Time	Peak Time	Ascent Duration

Descent Start Time	Finish Time	Descent Duration

Notes

Total Duration	Total Distance

Difficulty: [1] [2] [3] [4] [5] [6] [7] [8] [9] [10]
Views: [1] [2] [3] [4] [5] [6] [7] [8] [9] [10]

GREAT DODD
857 m / 2812 ft

Region	Eastern
OS Grid	NY342205
Parent Peak	Helvellyn

Date	Weather Condition

Ascent Start Time	Peak Time	Ascent Duration

Descent Start Time	Finish Time	Descent Duration

Notes

Total Duration	Total Distance

Difficulty: [1] [2] [3] [4] [5] [6] [7] [8] [9] [10]
Views: [1] [2] [3] [4] [5] [6] [7] [8] [9] [10]

DOLLYWAGGON PIKE
858 m / 2815 ft

Region		Eastern
OS Grid		NY346130
Parent Peak		Helvellyn

Date	Weather Condition

Ascent Start Time	Peak Time	Ascent Duration

Descent Start Time	Finish Time	Descent Duration

Notes

Total Duration	Total Distance

Difficulty ① ② ③ ④ ⑤ ⑥ ⑦ ⑧ ⑨ ⑩
Views ① ② ③ ④ ⑤ ⑥ ⑦ ⑧ ⑨ ⑩

TRINKLE CRAGS (LONG TOP)
859 m / 2818 ft

Region		Southern
OS Grid		NY248048
Parent Peak		Scafell Pike

Date	Weather Condition

Ascent Start Time	Peak Time	Ascent Duration

Descent Start Time	Finish Time	Descent Duration

Notes

Total Duration	Total Distance

Difficulty ① ② ③ ④ ⑤ ⑥ ⑦ ⑧ ⑨ ⑩
Views ① ② ③ ④ ⑤ ⑥ ⑦ ⑧ ⑨ ⑩

White Side
863 m / 2831 ft

Region	Eastern
OS Grid	NY337166
Parent Peak	Raise

Date	Weather Condition

Ascent Start Time	Peak Time	Ascent Duration

Descent Start Time	Finish Time	Descent Duration

Notes

	Total Duration	Total Distance
Difficulty	1 2 3 4 5 6 7 8 9 10	
Views	1 2 3 4 5 6 7 8 9 10	

Skiddaw Little Man
865 m / 2838 ft

Region	Northern
OS Grid	NY266277
Parent Peak	Skiddaw

Date	Weather Condition

Ascent Start Time	Peak Time	Ascent Duration

Descent Start Time	Finish Time	Descent Duration

Notes

	Total Duration	Total Distance
Difficulty	1 2 3 4 5 6 7 8 9 10	
Views	1 2 3 4 5 6 7 8 9 10	

BLENCATHRA (HALLSFELL TOP)
868 m / 2848 ft

Region	Northern
OS Grid	NY323277
Parent Peak	Skiddaw

Date	Weather Condition

Ascent Start Time	Peak Time	Ascent Duration

Descent Start Time	Finish Time	Descent Duration

Notes	Total Duration	Total Distance

Difficulty: (1) (2) (3) (4) (5) (6) (7) (8) (9) (10)
Views: (1) (2) (3) (4) (5) (6) (7) (8) (9) (10)

FAIRFIELD
873 m / 2864 ft

Region	Eastern
OS Grid	NY358117
Parent Peak	Helvellyn

Date	Weather Condition

Ascent Start Time	Peak Time	Ascent Duration

Descent Start Time	Finish Time	Descent Duration

Notes	Total Duration	Total Distance

Difficulty: (1) (2) (3) (4) (5) (6) (7) (8) (9) (10)
Views: (1) (2) (3) (4) (5) (6) (7) (8) (9) (10)

RAISE
883 m / 2897 ft

Region	Eastern
OS Grid	NY342174
Parent Peak	Helvellyn

Date	Weather Condition

Ascent Start Time	Peak Time	Ascent Duration

Descent Start Time	Finish Time	Descent Duration

Notes

Total Duration	Total Distance

Difficulty: 1 2 3 4 5 6 7 8 9 10
Views: 1 2 3 4 5 6 7 8 9 10

ESK PIKE
885 m / 2904 ft

Region	Southern
OS Grid	NY236075
Parent Peak	Bowfell

Date	Weather Condition

Ascent Start Time	Peak Time	Ascent Duration

Descent Start Time	Finish Time	Descent Duration

Notes

Total Duration	Total Distance

Difficulty: 1 2 3 4 5 6 7 8 9 10
Views: 1 2 3 4 5 6 7 8 9 10

Catstye Cam

890 m / 2920 ft

Region	Eastern
OS Grid	NY348158
Parent Peak	Helvellyn

Date	Weather Condition

Ascent Start Time	Peak Time	Ascent Duration

Descent Start Time	Finish Time	Descent Duration

Notes	Total Duration	Total Distance

Difficulty [1] [2] [3] [4] [5] [6] [7] [8] [9] [10]
Views [1] [2] [3] [4] [5] [6] [7] [8] [9] [10]

Nethermost Pike

891 m / 2923 ft

Region	Eastern
OS Grid	NY343142
Parent Peak	Helvellyn

Date	Weather Condition

Ascent Start Time	Peak Time	Ascent Duration

Descent Start Time	Finish Time	Descent Duration

Notes	Total Duration	Total Distance

Difficulty [1] [2] [3] [4] [5] [6] [7] [8] [9] [10]
Views [1] [2] [3] [4] [5] [6] [7] [8] [9] [10]

PILLAR
892 m / 2927 ft

Region	Western
OS Grid	NY171121
Parent Peak	Great Gable

Date | **Weather Condition**

Ascent Start Time | **Peak Time** | **Ascent Duration**

Descent Start Time | **Finish Time** | **Descent Duration**

Notes | **Total Duration** | **Total Distance**

Difficulty [1] [2] [3] [4] [5] [6] [7] [8] [9] [10]
Views [1] [2] [3] [4] [5] [6] [7] [8] [9] [10]

GREAT GABLE
899 m / 2949 ft

Region	Western
OS Grid	NY211103
Parent Peak	Scafell Pike

Date | **Weather Condition**

Ascent Start Time | **Peak Time** | **Ascent Duration**

Descent Start Time | **Finish Time** | **Descent Duration**

Notes | **Total Duration** | **Total Distance**

Difficulty [1] [2] [3] [4] [5] [6] [7] [8] [9] [10]
Views [1] [2] [3] [4] [5] [6] [7] [8] [9] [10]

BOWFELL
903 m / 2962 ft

Region	Southern
OS Grid	NY244064
Parent Peak	Scafell Pike

Date	Weather Condition

Ascent Start Time	Peak Time	Ascent Duration

Descent Start Time	Finish Time	Descent Duration

Notes	Total Duration	Total Distance

Difficulty: (1) (2) (3) (4) (5) (6) (7) (8) (9) (10)
Views: (1) (2) (3) (4) (5) (6) (7) (8) (9) (10)

GREAT END
910 m / 2984 ft

Region	Southern
OS Grid	NY226083
Parent Peak	Ill Crag

Date	Weather Condition

Ascent Start Time	Peak Time	Ascent Duration

Descent Start Time	Finish Time	Descent Duration

Notes	Total Duration	Total Distance

Difficulty: (1) (2) (3) (4) (5) (6) (7) (8) (9) (10)
Views: (1) (2) (3) (4) (5) (6) (7) (8) (9) (10)

SKIDDAW
931 m / 3054 ft

Region	Northern
OS Grid	NY260290
Parent Peak	

Date	Weather Condition

Ascent Start Time	Peak Time	Ascent Duration

Descent Start Time	Finish Time	Descent Duration

Notes	Total Duration	Total Distance

Difficulty: ① ② ③ ④ ⑤ ⑥ ⑦ ⑧ ⑨ ⑩
Views: ① ② ③ ④ ⑤ ⑥ ⑦ ⑧ ⑨ ⑩

HELVELLYN
950 m / 3117 ft

Region	Eastern
OS Grid	NY342151
Parent Peak	Scafell Pike

Date	Weather Condition

Ascent Start Time	Peak Time	Ascent Duration

Descent Start Time	Finish Time	Descent Duration

Notes	Total Duration	Total Distance

Difficulty: ① ② ③ ④ ⑤ ⑥ ⑦ ⑧ ⑨ ⑩
Views: ① ② ③ ④ ⑤ ⑥ ⑦ ⑧ ⑨ ⑩

SCAFELL
964 m / 3162 ft

Region	Southern
OS Grid	NY206064
Parent Peak	Scafell Pike

Date	Weather Condition

Ascent Start Time	Peak Time	Ascent Duration

Descent Start Time	Finish Time	Descent Duration

Notes	Total Duration	Total Distance

Difficulty: (1) (2) (3) (4) (5) (6) (7) (8) (9) (10)
Views: (1) (2) (3) (4) (5) (6) (7) (8) (9) (10)

SCAFELL PIKE
978 m / 3209 ft

Region	Southern
OS Grid	NY215072
Parent Peak	Snowdon

Date	Weather Condition

Ascent Start Time	Peak Time	Ascent Duration

Descent Start Time	Finish Time	Descent Duration

Notes	Total Duration	Total Distance

Difficulty: (1) (2) (3) (4) (5) (6) (7) (8) (9) (10)
Views: (1) (2) (3) (4) (5) (6) (7) (8) (9) (10)

Notes

Notes

Notes

Notes

Notes

Notes

Notes

Printed in Great Britain
by Amazon